PUSHED TO THE EDGE

How to Stop the

Child Competition Race

So Everyone Wins

DONNA G. CORWIN

Foreword by Dr. Jenn Berman

BERKLEY BOOKS, NEW YORK

B

A Berkley Book
Published by The Berkley Publishing Group
A division of Penguin Group (USA) Inc.
375 Hudson Street
New York, New York 10014

This book is an original publication of The Berkley Publishing Group.

Copyright © 2003 by Donna G. Corwin.
Cover design by Pyrographx.
Text design by Tiffany Estreicher.

PRINTING HISTORY
Berkley trade paperback edition / November 2003

Library of Congress Cataloging-in-Publication Data

Corwin, Donna G.
Pushed to the edge : how to stop the child competition race
so everyone wins / Donna G. Corwin.
p. cm.
ISBN 0-425-19186-9
1. Parenting. 2. Child rearing. 3. Competition (Psychology) in children.
4. Stress in children.   I. Title

HQ769.C7462   2003
649'.1—dc21
2003051815

PRINTED IN THE UNITED STATES OF AMERICA

10 9 8 7 6 5 4 3 2 1

To Alexandra—my precious daughter.
You push me to be a better parent.

To Stan—my husband and mentor.
You always believe in me.

ACKNOWLEDGMENTS

My deepest and most sincere gratitude go to those people whose encouragement, contributions, and insights were invaluable while I was writing this book.

Denise Silvestro—An amazing editor, who "pushed me to the edge" in the best possible ways and whose suggestions and changes were invaluable in shaping the book.

Jane Dystel—My agent, who always believed in the book, championed it, and guided the process.

Ann Benya—Computer genius and great lady who kept the pages flying. Thank you.

Dr. Jill Model Barth, Terry Gopadze, Dr. Jenn Berman, and Shirley Gram—Thank you for your psychological insights and perspectives, your generosity and special friendships.

Thank you to all of the parents and children who talked to me about their fears, vulnerabilities, and feelings about competition. You were the foundation of *Pushed to the Edge*.

CONTENTS

AUTHOR'S NOTE

The purpose of *Pushed to the Edge* is to foster understanding and awareness of the roots of competition and show how competition can be utilized in a positive as opposed to a negative way. I have stumbled over my own parenting mistakes, and in an effort to learn how to become a better parent, I have realized how I have pushed my child too far, too fast. There is nothing about parenting that is set in stone because people are too changeable, too unpredictable, and too diverse. But over the years, I have noticed the push to compete has intensified, as if parents were in a one-upsmanship race with one another. After talking with hundreds of children and teenagers, I am convinced that most of them are feeling the stressors of a society that too quickly casts aside kids who can't keep up with the furious pace. Those who can keep up are so overwhelmed with work that they typically face burnout.

Parents are victims as well, because they are afraid if they don't push their child, he might miss some amorphous opportunities and advancements. Our society has become conditioned, placing too much emphasis on the "right" school, the "right" college, the "right" friends. In truth, the only thing that is right is a loving relationship with your child, a happy well-adjusted child with good interpersonal skills, and a child who feels good about himself. This is the best recipe for success.

FOREWORD
BY DR. JENN BERMAN

Megan, a teenage ice skater, came into my psychotherapy and sports psychology office because her mother had heard I worked with her daughter's competitor and her score had improved after only two sessions. During my initial interview with the teen, I asked about her strengths and weaknesses as an athlete, her training regimen, and the most formidable impediments to her upcoming competition season. Megan told me that her coach and her mom had been concerned about her weight ever since she turned thirteen. When I asked what she was doing to control her weight, she replied matter-of-factly, "I've been throwing up." I asked if her parents knew, and she replied, "Yes. When I told my mother, she told me to do whatever it takes to win."

While that experience is an extreme example, I have noticed a trend over the past few years of parents pushing their children harder and harder to achieve academic, athletic, and extracurricular perfection. Many parents are surprised to learn that not just the elite athletes are feeling pressured, but the "regular" kids are as well. Parents often do not realize that they are not only pushing too hard, but that there are extreme emotional and physical tolls this stress places on their children. I have seen a dramatic increase in children who are burned out, overscheduled, and feeling pressured to be the "perfect" child. Younger and younger children are coming into my office with problems of depression, anxiety, and eating disorders. Many of them feel that they have already lost their childhoods and that their lives are just one big competitive test.

Pushed to the Edge: How to Stop the Child Competition Race So Everyone Wins could not have come at a better time. The number of parents who are pushing their kids too hard is reaching epidemic proportions. Everyone wants the best for his child, but before Donna Corwin wrote this book, there was no manual to assist parents in figuring out how to do that. Her book will help parents bridge the fine line between helping their children live up to their fullest potential and pushing them so hard that their ability to succeed is destroyed.

In her book, Donna focuses on the pressures today's youth face in academics, sports, beauty, and social status. Unfortunately, I have yet to see a child who has not been affected by the stresses he or she has faced in at least one of these areas. Most kids today feel tremendous pressure to look and perform a certain way. If the burden does not come from their parents, it often comes from their teachers, coaches, and peers. This makes the parent's task doubly challenging: to help their sons and daughters cope with the pressure to perform they receive from outside of the home, and to resist the temptation to add their own pressures from within the home.

Donna really writes from her heart. She is an experienced author who has written six bestselling books on parenting in addition to hundreds of articles on the topic. She has an amazing ability to place her finger on the pulse of the parenting community and to use her own wealth of knowledge as a parent. And she is an exceptional parent who is never afraid to expose her own frailties in order to help others learn from her mistakes.

I have spent the last twenty-three years in many diverse roles. I am a licensed psychotherapist who works with adults, children, couples, and families. I also work as a sports psychology consultant. In addition, I have been a member of the USA Gymnastics Task Force on the Female Triad (eating disorders, amenorrhea, and osteoporosis), as well as a sports psychology consultant and advisor to USA Gymnastics on the Athlete Wellness Task Force. I perform consulting services for A Minor Consideration, an organization begun by child actor Paul Petersen, which looks out for the well-being of child actors and athletes. I have served as a sports coach, a judge for gymnastic competitions, and I grew up as an elite level athlete. I spent five years on the United States Rhythmic Gymnastics National Team, was a Junior National Champion, winning five gold medals out of five, competed in many international competitions and performed exhibitions at the 1984 Olympic Games.

As a result of all this work, I have seen the best and the

worst effects of competition on children. At its best, participation in sports has the ability to increase self-esteem, create a sense of self-efficacy, to teach a child to overcome failure, help develop sportsmanship, discipline, master new physical skills, and overcome adversity. At its worst, sports can leave a child feeling like a failure and questioning his own identity and abilities.

In *Pushed to the Edge,* Donna presents a balanced approach to childhood participation in activities while examining the healthy aspects of competition. This book will help parents create a strong parent-child relationship, allowing children the opportunity to thrive. Too many parents seek out books to help their son or daughter become an über child, but it is the exceptional parent who will pick up a guide like this to learn how to form a loving relationship with their child while helping him or her to feel supported and accepted. I believe this book will help parents achieve the best of both worlds. I commend you for taking the first step toward helping your child cope with the pressures of the world we live in today.

Dr. Jenn Berman
Psychotherapist
Sports Psychology Consultant
www.DoctorJenn.com

INTRODUCTION

Karen was thrilled to report that her fifteen-year-old had doubled his birthday money by picking stocks on the Internet. Karen's friends were amazed and even begged her son to help their children learn about stocks. Karen told the parents about a new summer camp for kids, "Help Your Child Become a Millionaire," a program that teaches kids about stocks, bonds, and finances. The twelve-hundred-dollar-a-week camp was filled within a few weeks, with a long waiting list. Obviously, the camp director had followed his own advice. When another friend, Lois, told the same group of friends about her daughter's charitable work with the homeless, she was greeted with, "Oh, how nice," but the conversation quickly turned back to a request for stock tips from Karen's son.

When Johnny's mother declared he was reading by age three, David's mother was ready to call an educational specialist because poor David could barely get through *The Little Engine That Could* at age five. She was sure he was learning-disabled.

Ben was told his chances for college were dim because his B's and C's in high school and lack of sports talent put him in the category of "average," and average in today's competitive society is thought to be academic failure.

Alan took out a bank loan so he could pay a soccer coach five hundred dollars a week to work with his son—his ten-year-old son. Alan's rationale was, "Start him young, he'll play varsity, and hopefully get a scholarship to college or, better yet, make it to the Olympics." Alan had lofty goals for a boy who admitted he didn't really even like soccer that much.

Pushed to the Edge explores and analyzes the parental and societal race to push children into the competition arena. It looks at the ways in which early competition can negatively affect the parent-child relationship and how destructive competition can damage children. The book shows how to foster positive, constructive, and healthy competition.

As a concerned parent, writer, and lecturer, I constantly hear pleas from other worried parents who feel trapped in the competition race. If a child does not meet almost unattainable standards, he feels unworthy—not good enough. As a generation that preaches "self-esteem," we may be in danger of pushing our children over the edge. The end result may be not only the loss of a child's sense of worth, but a loss of his childhood.

Pushed to the Edge explores today's child—an overprogrammed, overstimulated, overcompetitive little being who may be navigating the Internet by age two, trading online by six, and running a company by sixteen. It also includes an in-depth exploration of the competitive parental drive, where it comes from, and how it can be used in a loving, positive way.

The book looks at our fast-paced society and how it feeds the frenzy of competition. The images of "super" models, godlike athletes, techno-geniuses, and boy/girl wonders are everywhere in the media. After speaking with high school kids from different areas and backgrounds, I learned they no longer want to work at McDonald's or the Gap for weekend and summer jobs. They aspire to internships at law firms, film studios, and Internet companies.

This greatly contrasts with the previous generation, where young people were applauded and rewarded for working in the Peace Corps and programs like Head Start. Parents took pride in these altruistic accomplishments of their children. Today, the measure of success is in "big" money and power.

Anxious parents who feel an overwhelming need to push their children into the competitive arena are paying a high price for their ambitions. Parents who are panicked if their toddler doesn't get into the "right nusery school" and parents who spend thousands of dollars for tutors and special programs to prep their teen for the S.A.T. are creating anxiety-ridden children. Many of these children are burning out: some develop medical and emotional problems; some merely decide they've had enough and rebel by dropping out of everything. These burned-out kids rarely go on to college and lose the drive and self-esteem necessary for a happy, successful life.

Competition is defined in the dictionary as a "vying with others; a struggle." This "struggle" is carried out routinely as part of the parenting process by caring, loving parents who are fearful their child will somehow be left behind everyone else. But in truth, it is the parents, not the child, who are competing. Childhood should be a happy, easygoing time of exploration and learning for the sake of learning. Instead, children have become social weapons in our competitive society. We use our children's accomplishments to bolster our social position. We think the schools they go to, the clothes they wear, and the trophies they get reflect how successful we are as parents. Children are pawns, and if the push to compete does not slow down, children will lose their innocence and simply shut down. We all want what's best for our kids, but each generation sets a standard of "best"— and today the barrier may be raised too high. Children are finding it more and more difficult to reach the unrealistic standards set by society. Children need to have their own dreams, and our role as parents is to encourage and support them.

The alarming statistics suggest that approximately 5 percent of the children in the United States have attention deficit hyperactivity disorder (ADHD) and almost 10 percent have learning disabilities. One explanation is that we are more aware of these learning differences now and, therefore, diagnose them more frequently. Another thought is that many of these children are "normal," but because the competitive bar has been raised so much higher now, many fall short of the expectations planned for them. Needless to say, a child with problems should be offered help, but, more often than not, many of these children are marginalized in the system because they cannot measure up to the new norm.

Pushed to the Edge also looks at healthy competition. Competition can be positive if presented in a way that helps a child build self-confidence, teaches fair sportsmanship, and creates a good self-image. But if the role models chosen by parent and child are unworthy (anorexic magazine supermodels, violent sports heroes, drug-abusing, misogynistic music stars), and build on values of money and power, then a child can get a distorted view of what's important in life.

Goals should be set for each individual, not by using some across-the-board set of standards. "You should be rich, famous, pretty, and smart." These are empty in themselves. They should only be by-products of healthy values, kindness, generosity, love of family and friends, creative and intellectual pursuits. Not every child will be pretty, smart, or talented. Parents need to find each child's "specialness" and nurture it. By doing so, the child will find his own way and feel empowered as a person. Competition will be internal, not based on external false expectations.

Pushed to the Edge will help parents trace the generational roots of competition and gives an overview of the different arenas of competition: academic, sports, beauty, weight issues, social, and parent-to-parent.

Probably one of the most painful discoveries in my life was finding out that my daughter had a learning disability. She would never be able to get the straight A's I received in school. She would have to work harder than all of her friends. My child would never "compete" in this arena where the competition among her peers was fierce. To listen to other parents, you might believe that every child is gifted and destined for Ivy League colleges. Academically, my child was not. Still, I pushed her, believing she could measure up if she studied harder, longer. The stress was tearing our family apart.

How could a competitive person like myself become humble about my daughter in the face of this information? Would people think less of me if my daughter was not academically a star?

Ironically, it took the brilliant insight of my child to set me straight, to knock some sense into her pushy mother. One day, after chastising her for a poor grade on a test she gave her all to, she said emphatically, "I'm much more than grades and tests, Mom. I'm not in competition with anyone.

I'll be successful because I feel good about who I am. Stop pushing me. Stop wanting what I can't give you."

After the shock wore off and I quit reeling from these profound words of maturity from a young adolescent, I let it all sink in. The parental competition was so strong in me and in the community we lived in, that I had fallen into the trap of "pushing" for good grades. I couldn't see the whole child, but rather focused on a singular measure of success—a grade on a test. I wasn't looking at my child's needs, but rather my own. There was no doubt that this girl, who was so comfortable in her own skin, would be successful. I began to see her humor, her creativity, her curiosity, her social and sports skills. I began to nurture rather than push, and our relationship became closer.

After writing seven parenting books and countless articles, I have had the opportunity to talk to hundreds of parents. They told me about their fears, frustrations, and desires. One of parents' overriding concerns is how the competitive push can actually hurt the family unit. It is clear that parents are torn between what they think they should do for their children because of the societal "push" to get ahead, and what they know in their hearts is the right thing to do. Parents are tired of the race. But they don't know how to stop.

My hope is that parents will take the time to reflect on how their child is being affected by parental and societal pushing. Learn how to foster healthy competition and break free of negative patterns of behavior that prevent you and your child from having a truly positive and bonded relationship.

Ultimately, *Pushed to the Edge* will help the parent value his or her child for all he or she is. Children are not us. They are their own special, wonderful selves. We must allow them to make mistakes—even fail. Their successes and failures build character and determination. The business of parenting is not based on competition. It is rooted in love. Who can compete with that?

1

THE NEED TO COMPETE

Why We Compete

Why do humans compete? Is it human nature? Going back to the beginning of the human species, man only existed by "survival of the fittest." Humans had to compete for food, shelter, and the affections of a mate. As time progressed, we adopted a social hierarchy with customs and traditions, but there was still the innate drive to have the better hut, castle, or cave. Survival drives exist, but for some, the drive goes beyond survival and more toward competition. Instead of a hut or cave, these people strive for mansions and luxury cars, the better position at work, to be known as the prettiest, thinnest, strongest, smartest, and funniest. These innate drives to better ourselves are normal until they start to impact relationships and we become willing to push others aside for our own gain, when the things we accumulate are no longer about need but rather about having the "most," whether it be the most shoes, cars, purses, watches, or toys. Even fundraising for charity has become based on competition. The most lucrative charity events are runs, walks, bike rides, and marathons—activities in which there is a designated winner.

Clearly, animals compete to live. In order to get food to survive, animals must use their strength and cunning. This is especially true in lion prides where the males fight over and compete for the females. Weaker animals are often pushed out of the pride or killed. The most colorful peacock gets the girl. With humans, the wealthiest, most powerful man often gets the girl. There is a similarity in that animals and humans need to attract the opposite sex in order to propagate the species, and competition plays a role in this. But once animals mate, they move on to attend to their next need. Animals are instinctive. Their competition is based on survival.

Humans, in contrast, very frequently continue "vying with others" well beyond actual need. We have even built societies with a hierarchy based on who has the most "things." This system establishes classes. The class system is exclusionary in that if you can't compete—with money, looks, power, brains—you will remain on the lower rungs of the class ladder. Winning becomes a psychological one-upsmanship. This is shown by sports competition or beauty contests. Humans often compete for the sake of winning. Competition can function to buoy up your ego by another's loss. The winner can let people know he is first. This is exemplified by the reality shows that create celebrities out of people who win popularity contests with the public. There is a great deal of satisfaction because winning makes us feel superior.

An animal will nurture its young, then set them free, where ultimately they will survive or perish. Humans are unique because many of them often do not accept their children "as is." They mold, measure, push, prod, alter, accept, reject, and compete for the top spot in the jungle. The trouble is, there are so many parents trying to get their child on the top branch of the tree, that it is in danger of snapping. No one seems to just grow up anymore. There is a long list of do's, don'ts, and must-haves in order to survive in the human jungle, which can be more difficult than the animal one.

In his book *Competing*, psychiatrist Dr. Harvey L. Ruben asserts that we have a genetic code that is programmed toward competition. Added to this inherited component is what we are taught and what we experience. From the time a child is an infant, Dr. Ruben says, he develops "unintentional competitiveness." He is constantly being gratified. The child acts naturally out of need because he can't satisfy himself. The parent nurtures and gives the child what he wants usually without delay, and before other members of the family's needs are met, proving that "nurture" and "nature" are acting hand in hand. By toddlerhood, the child's competitiveness is intentional by his drive to win the toy, the attention, the cookie. He knows certain actions (crying, whining) will get him a reaction—over a sibling or other children. Oftentimes, we compete solely for attention, whether it be negative or positive. By the time the child is in school, comparisons are being made daily by the grade a child receives, his popularity, his sports ability. If the genetic component were all there was, then we could say a noncompetitive, passive parent would have a noncompetitive, passive child. But this idea does not always prove to be true. There is controversy between the "nature" and "nurture" schools of thought, but the latter seems to be most pervasive currently.

Between the ages of four and six years old, a child is cognizant of the roles his mother and father play in his life. Therefore, he becomes unconsciously jealous in the knowledge that he will have to share his mother with his father. He starts to compete for their attention, and often will whine or act out to get his way. This is a time when parents need to establish a united front, and not let the toddler pull them apart. Eventually he will separate from each. The separation stage is painful but normal.

Many children are separating, physically, earlier from

mothers who are in the workforce. The child learns early on in play groups and preschool that in order to get "attention," he has to compete with other children who have the same immediate wants and needs. The shy introverted child is often left on his own. Many parents who feel guilty because of their unavailability will push daycare workers or nannies to make sure their child is getting enough attention. As the child grows, he learns how to push in front of others, grab his toy, and whine for what he wants. These are lessons of life that start when some children are not even walking. If a child is constantly gratified without any delay, he is incapable of self-soothing. He will push others because he can't wait. This sounds unfortunate, yet some maintain that even competition whose driving force seems unfavorable helps children learn to adapt to present-day society and that the early lessons of competition assure self-reliance.

According to Dr. Ruben, "Children who fail to learn *how* to compete early in life develop emotional problems later on." In his view, successful competitors are healthier because they can keep their egos intact even if they lose. Therefore, the key is learning how to compete rather than how to win. It is inevitable that children will learn to play competitive games and will at some point lose. It is the way we teach them to play, to win, and to lose that forms the basis of their character.

Dr. Ruben asserts that, central to competition are the lessons parents teach about it. Probably the most important one is *when to walk away*. Helping a child learn his strengths and weaknesses may be the best lesson you ever teach. Why? Because you are fostering your child's self-esteem by allowing him to accept his limitations.

It can be surmised that early competition can lead to aggressive behavior. The parents who push children to compete too early and "win at all costs" can be fostering overly aggressive behavior. Very young children do not have an understanding of the nuances of healthy competition—team play, fairness, personal best—and act out inappropriately not only to win but also to please the parents. If early aggressions are not channeled positively, then they can lead to unhealthy behaviors such as violence and social maladaptiveness. Children become aggressive when they do not have boundaries. Therefore, the need to compete should be channeled in a positive and healthy way and at an appropriate age. Toddlers should be learning to socialize and share, not to be the first or to have the best building blocks. Let's try to understand what is the societal influence of competition.

The Starting Line

According to psychologist Dr. Jill Model Barth, we compete because we can. Baby Boomers have more money, education, and accessibility than previous generations. Thus, as Dr. Barth points out, "People are given the idea by both the social media and financial circumstance that anyone can achieve whatever they want." We live by the ethos that anything is possible, and this idea of limitless possibility extends to our children. Any suggestion to a parent that his child can't "be it all," "do it all," or "have it all" is tantamount to an emotional attack.

This same belief compels parents to push children beyond what their capabilities are. The irony is that when children are pushed to compete in areas in which they are not comfortable, they will often shut down. The parents who wanted their child to have a good sense of self often find a withdrawn, burned-out child who feels less than successful because she simply cannot compete in the arena that she has been pushed into.

As society has become more educated and affluent, the bar has been raised. Today's children must be better, smarter, prettier, more well behaved. And well-intentioned parents, wanting their children to achieve all they can, are pushing even harder. As a result, these kids are growing up overstimulated and overprogrammed; their time is too structured and their activities too supervised. Their lives have no free form. Rather, parents create a "master plan." This plan usually includes an expensive education, music and dance lessons, computer lessons, karate, soccer, tennis, swimming, cooking classes, and, most recently, financial planning. Children have no time for idle play, which is considered wasted time. The "hang out and do nothing" attitude of previous generations is anathema to today's society.

There is a kind of "frantic" feeling that grips parents. Quiet time, which used to mean playing games or just daydreaming, is now considered goofing off. If a parent sees a child staring into space, she may equate it with boredom. Time in our competitive society is seen as a precious commodity that must be used wisely and filled up productively or your child might not achieve all that you dream for her. Your job as a competitive parent has become well defined—work fifty hours or more a week, then chauffeur the kids, cook, clean, help with homework, coach soccer, and on and on. Certainly there is no time to just "hang out." Everything has a function and a purpose. There is a race to "get" and not just to "be."

The core family is broken up into subgroups—all doing something else. Mom is working late, Billy has soccer practice, Kirstin is at dance class, Dad has a work project and no time for dinner. Everyone grabs something and dinner is on the run. Whatever happened to the days of the family talks around the dinner table? This is where wisdom, wit, and values were explored and discussed. Children today are now learning ideas and values from external as opposed to internal sources. They now get their information from classes and coaches more than from Mom and Dad. The heart of family life is being lost.

David Brooks, author of *Bobos in Paradise,* is a chronicler of the overachieving "Boomlets" (children of Baby Boomers) who, for the most part, are bright, hard-working, and social. So what's to complain about? Doesn't every parent want a child who is successful, talented, athletic, bright?

The downside, Brooks notes, is that "we may be robbing our children of the experience of being children because of both our inability to let our children fall, bang and scrape themselves, and because parents avert any chance of child failure by avoiding risk at all costs."

Parents can become so preoccupied with their child's future that they live with constant anxiety about the present. They may become worried to the point of stifling the child in the present to protect his future. As Brooks says, "a broken arm, once a badge of courageous rambunctious play, is now seen as a child whose college baseball career might be endangered because of a slow-to-heal arm. Thus, we have the parent who, even as his child is wanting to be a little wild, a little gregarious, puts the brakes on for fear that something will happen so he can no longer compete."

Therefore, you have a society of anxious parents and overworked children who are competing, but for what?

Entitlement

One reason we compete is because we think we and our children are entitled to. Boomers who have worked hard and benefited from their parents' years of scrimping and saving have the attitude they can—and should—have it all and their children "must" only have the best of everything. Children adopt this philosophy of entitlement and embrace the idea that the good life is theirs for the taking.

This mindset of "having it all" may have actually started in the post-Depression era, when parents wanted their children to have everything they were denied. When the economy improved after the war, these parents were able to give their children "everything." As a result of the postwar boom, more Americans had a house, a car, and the opportunity to make money. And the more money people made, the more they spent. As television ushered in advertising in a new media, we became a society of avid consumers. The measure of success was marked by how many things one had—a fur coat, jewelry, a big car. If John had a big house, Joe wanted one too. People soon went into debt trying to keep up. Fear grips many people when they think they might not be able to afford as much as their friends and neighbors. Somehow, a lack of things makes people feel diminished. These feelings are what cause people to become debtors. This childish "keeping up with the Joneses" attitude carried over into the next generation.

The Baby Boomers are a group who long ago forgot their childhood roots of marches and protests, experimentation and unstructured time. They have been coddled in adulthood into an expectation that everyone has a big house, two cars, and vacations every summer. Credit cards and the advertising media fed their hunger and hooked an entire generation on "material goods."

And what these Baby Boomers coveted, so would their children. In fact, the Boomers viewed their children as an extension of themselves; therefore, these children had to reflect the athleticism and intelligence and sophistication of their parents. Today's children are the progeny of a class society that measures prep schools and scholarships like identifying birthmarks. Ski vacations and cruises have become de rigueur. Children, along with their parents, believe "they deserve it."

But for some people, a house, two cars, and a yearly vacation are not enough. Power-hungry executives like Michael Milkin, Kenneth Lay of Enron, and Gary Winnick of Global Crossing couldn't amass enough money to make themselves happy. They wanted power as well. For them, using other peoples' money became a game. These greed barons began to compete with one another—leaving the rest of the working class to eat dust with not so much as an apology for all of their corporate misdeeds.

Thus, the corporate competitor was born—the person who made billions, but forgot to take care of the people whose billions they were spending. Many of our children are the product of greed barons, whose message is "more," "bigger," "best." Children are getting the message that anything less makes them less. And this belief has filtered down to the masses.

For these reasons, parents make a serious effort to provide their child with an abundance of things starting in infancy. There are designer car seats, Mommy and Me classes that cost as much as college, Gucci diaper bags, and nannies whose salaries are way above that of teachers. These are not just the must-haves of the idle rich. These have become the must-haves of the middle class, and even those families who are financially squeezed strive to make sure their children have enough toys and designer tennis shoes.

Our society is outwardly based on competition. We are no longer competing for food and shelter. It is the desire to "show off what we have" that pushes Western culture to the edge. The competitive symbols of status are exclusive, not inclusive. The more we compete for symbols, the more we teach our children to exclude others. If we achieve something, we look down on those who have not. This attitude forms the basis of prejudice, snobbery, and feelings of superiority.

Entitlement has historically caused the downfall of governments and created such noticeable players as Czar Nicholas of Russia, who, along with his family, was assassinated in an effort to kill off the rich aristocracy; Marie Antoinette, who, living in lavish luxury, was reputed to have shown great disdain for the poor and starving; and Imelda Marcos, who was chided for owning hundreds of shoes and flaunting her wealth while her people starved.

Similarly, in our present-day society, companies such as Worldcom and Adelphia have crashed and burned because their competitive CEOs felt their position put them above their employees, and essentially above the law. They did not have a conscience about what was good for society and their employees, but rather were only concerned about where they were positioned on the competition ladder.

This sense of entitlement led these corporate titans into a deluded sense of who they were. They viewed their workers as expendable, whose purpose was to serve their needs. When we fall prey to greed and power, we corrupt our society. The tenets of fairness, equality, and team spirit are lost when a few feel superior to the many. This entitlement is no longer about winning, but about winning *at all costs,* and, as witnessed throughout history, the cost can hurt us all.

Humans are constantly competing for grades, social position, friends, money, power. Competition is a mirror to our life which reflects our sense of identity and our social relationships to others. In today's world, we compete to gain one up on the other person. But this is a false sense of pride because it is fleeting as soon as the next person shows up with more.

What we teach our children about why we compete and how we compete, as well as how to avoid the dangers of the push of parental competition, is the focus of this book. It should guide you into lessons for your child and, maybe more importantly, lessons for yourself.

2

DIMINISHED EXPECTATIONS

Parental Approval

Some children will never live up to their parents' expectations. Ironically, what we expect from our children is often unrealistic. Parents may fantasize about having a superkid who excels academically, socially, athletically, and creatively. When a child falls short of these expectations, some parents show disapproval, sometimes by pulling away love and attention, which may cause a child to feel unloved and fearful. This type of behavior is manipulative and treads on dangerous ground. You can damage a child's trust in the parental bond if he doesn't feel he can make mistakes or fail without a parent disapproving. This bond is what gives your child a sense of security, trust, and confidence in the world.

When Bruce was younger, there was very little he could accomplish to get his father's approval. Bruce was a quiet, introverted child. His father was a boisterous type-A personality who constantly berated his son. He called Bruce a weakling in the hopes of "making him more macho." Bruce became angrier and angrier at his father. Bruce retreated further into a shell and needed long-term therapy to overcome his feelings of inadequacy. The guilt associated with disappointing a parent is overwhelming.

Children look for parental approval in a mother's smile, an affectionate hug, a dad's pat on the back, words of praise. All of this positive input is what helps form a child's sense of self. "If my parents think I'm okay, I must be." This is the internal unconscious cognitive dialogue that goes on in a child's mind.

If a child is to develop confidence and the ability to satisfy his needs without building competitive defenses, he must be able to begin to develop an ego. He must have a sense of self apart from the parental reflection. This ego strength is what helps a child to cope and attain self-reliance as he moves through life. If a child is continually pushed to compete and live up to parental approval, he won't be able to become self-secure and discover his individuality. He will always live under the shadow of comparison.

Childhood Passages

There are stages a child needs to go through in order to separate, individuate, and mature. Parents often push too hard to bypass certain stages in an effort to gain a competitive edge over others. Children reach these stages, sometimes earlier than others, but the healthy child is allowed to individuate at his own pace.

According to renowned developmental psychologist Dr. Margaret Mahler, a child's sense of self and security begins in infancy. Her published research and theory of development have chronicled the various stages that lead to parent-child separation—individuation. This separation is necessary in order for the child to gain a sense of autonomy and mastery over his world. It is also important for the parents, so they do not smother and overidentify with their child. This especially holds true for the mother, who establishes the primary physical bond in infancy.

During the *Symbiotic Stage,* birth to two months, the infant is fused with the mother. He does not view himself as separate from the mother, but rather an extension of her. It is important during this stage that the mother meet all of the infant's needs without frustrating the child because the baby has no sense of the world beyond his mother. The child competes unconsciously at this stage to get his mother's attention so his needs are met. For this reason, early bonding is vital to healthy growth and attachment in infancy.

Between two to six months, the *Differential Stage* takes place. During this time, the child is becoming aware of his external surroundings. He needs visual and verbal stimulation, but remains fused with the parent, not ready to separate. He is continuing to bond, but will receive stimuli from other people. At this stage, the child may have to work harder to compete for the mother's attention.

At seven to eighteen months, during the *Practicing Stage,* the child directs his energy outward. He is so excited by his own abilities, including crawling, standing, and walking, that he is able to separate temporarily from the parent in order to explore his surroundings. The parent needs to be encouraging; the baby should feel safe so that he is unafraid to try new tasks. If the parent pushes too much at this stage, the child may become fearful and regress. It is important that at this stage the child feel no sense of competition, but rather the freedom to experiment. No two children will walk or crawl at the exact same age. Recognize that there is a developmentally appropriate age, but if your child walks at thirteen months and your friend's child walks at ten months, it does not mean one child is more advanced.

During the *Reapproachment Stage,* better known as toddlerhood, until age two, the child is conflicted between independence and regression to pre-separation. Many children at this stage will not leave their mother's side when there are other people around. But as soon as the toddler has her mother alone, she will test her independence and often be uncooperative. She'll want to dress herself, comb her own hair, and tend to things she is still too young to manage. The toddler should be watched and directed toward trying new tasks. Separation should never be forced, but gently encouraged. If a child is pushed too much, she may act out or pull back.

At the end of the Reapproachment Stage, the child should feel separate from the parent. If there is arrested development or infant trauma during one of these stages, it can have an influence on later emotional or psychological growth of the child.

This was evidenced in the case of Ron, age fifteen, who wanted to stop playing competitive tennis. His mother, Veronica, would not allow Ron to quit. Veronica had always babied her son—never separating her ego from his. She became hysterical at the thought of Ron not competing. In truth, it was Veronica who always wanted the adulation but did not have the athletic talent. She was never encouraged by her own mother.

Ron didn't know how to tell his mother he wanted "out." He wanted to separate from his mother but was too fearful to confront her. Every time Ron played poorly because he was lacking the drive, his mother detected this and badgered him further. Ron started experimenting with drugs as a way to detach. He ended up in the hospital.

Obviously, there were serious separation issues that carried over from infancy. Both mother and child were so enmeshed that neither could establish autonomy. His mother smothered Ron, pushing him into a sport that *she* loved. She assumed that he would want what she wanted. Ron had to come close to the edge in order to break free of his mother's hold on him.

Children whose parents push too much will act out in order to gain autonomy. By psychologically killing or hurting themselves, they are figuratively killing off the parental figure. Children are not capable of telling a parent or authority figure to back off. They are fearful of parental disapproval. It is important to read negative signals from your children and to know when they are trying to communicate.

The following illustrates some of the negative signs that a child gives a parent. These signals should be heeded. Your child is trying to tell you how he feels and needs your attention.

- Acting out emotionally (yelling, crying)

- Getting depressed (regressing, talking less, eating and sleeping problems)

- Refusing to take part in an activity

- Hurting himself physically

- Starting to perform poorly either at school or in an activity

These signals are a call for help. They imply, "I'm not happy. I need you to stop pushing me so much."

Today's parents rush to put young toddlers into baby programs, gym programs, and various classes, wanting their child to keep up with other toddlers. This apprehensive parent competition may get in the way of the child's inclination to develop naturally by trial and error. A child should be allowed to explore his world without a parent pushing him beyond his developmental capabilities. A timid child might not be ready to leave Mom's side. This child may want to go slower, progress on his own time. Parents tend to make too many comparisons—leading to competition with other young children. The child can start to feel anxious and/or fearful because he is afraid of displeasing his mother and making a mistake. You can attend any toddler group and observe a parent prodding her child to do a myriad of directed activities. "If Johnny goes down the slide, so can you." "Go on, go! Jump through the circle. All the other kids are doing it." "Why don't you swing like Susie?" All this direction may stifle the child's natural curiosity and actually impede the learning process. Children need to feel free to explore and learn without fear of criticism.

Parents think they are doing something positive by engaging

PASSAGES THROUGH PHYSICAL, INTELLECTUAL, SOCIAL, AND EMOTIONAL CHANGES

	TODDLERHOOD (2–4 years)	EARLY CHILDHOOD (5–8 years)
PHYSICAL CHANGES	• Physical developing—fine and gross motor skills • Physical play with toys	• There is more control over body—balance, movement, athletic skills • Boys and girls both physically active
INTELLECTUAL CHANGES	• By four, some children recognize numbers, letters, colors; write their names	• Reading, writing, and developing more complex skills
SOCIAL CHANGES	• Beginning social interaction in preschool, daycare, and with neighborhood friends • Learning boundaries	• Using imaginative play • Creating friendships • Teasing opposite sex • Learning rules
EMOTIONAL CHANGES	• Trepidation and excitement • Awareness of larger world	• Nightmares and fears common • Separation issues arise

YOUNG ADOLESCENCE (8–10 years)	EMERGING ADOLESCENCE (10–14 years)
• Puberty begins in many, particularly girls • Boys' height stable	• Girls start menstruating; develop breasts • Boys develop pubic hair; growth spurt at fourteen
• Handle homework, tests, projects • Spend more time working independently	• Authority and parental values are challenged • School is more competitive and complex • Higher-order thinking skills develop
• Cliques may begin to form, exclude others • Fascinated with anything "teen" (media, older siblings) • Organized sports may appeal	• Sexual awareness and growing flirtations with boyfriends/girlfriends • Experimentation with fashion, hair, appearance
• Worries center on self, friendships, solving "friend" problems, pleasing adults *other* than parents • Desire to please at school	• Worries about social status, family, health issues, family issues (death and dying), personal safety • Vulnerable to outside influences; peers take on tremendous importance

their children in many activities, but in actuality, the parents are investing their own egos in the process. The parental inner thought is, "My child is a reflection of me." In truth, your child may be similar to you in many ways, but in order to grow and thrive, he must distinguish himself from his parents and learn to survive on his own. His mistakes and failures are how a child learns. But many parents are overly involved and fearful of their child failing because they think it makes them look like a failure as parents.

If you continue to control your child's life, he will always look to you for not only approval, but validation. Instead, the child should be able to soothe and control himself in order to develop a healthy sense of self. A child needs to learn to please himself, not just his parents.

There is a difference between wanting the best for our kids and demanding the best, because the "best" means something different to each person. Our competitive society has set the best at a high level—a level that most of us will never attain, and even if we attain "the best," the bar rises again with time, age, and circumstance. Therefore, can we expect our children to attain what is out of reach for us? Did you reach further than your parents? Was it through your inner drive—or theirs? Did you go into the family business but would have rather become an artist? Are you the dancer whose mother dreamed of stardom, when what you really wanted to do was become a teacher?

A twelve-year-old boy may have amazing talent in sports, but he may be ten years old emotionally and perhaps eleven intellectually. The talent to kick a ball farther or jump higher is more realized when the athlete has the emotional intelligence to use focus, strategy, determination, and humility wisely. It is the blending of these passages that creates a well-rounded child and, inevitably, a better athlete. Tiger Woods's father, Earl Woods, agrees. He believes his son is 60 percent intelligence and emotional determination and 40 percent sports talent.

The chart on pages 22–23 sets out the childhood passages that children experience as they mature. Although not set in stone, these changes represent the norm in most children.

Sibling Rivalry

Parents often create competition between siblings. Parents use "favorites" with their children to get things done at home. Many parents believe it is the sibling competition that spurs children on to success—that comparing siblings motivates them. Faith always yells at her son Brett, "Your brother always cleans his room so well and is polite. Why aren't you the same?"

But this tactic can backfire. It sets up an unhealthy competition between siblings, and often one will overcompensate, and the other, feeling unworthy, will underperform.

This divisiveness creates an inner competition between siblings. There is a contest for the parents' attention. Love becomes seen as a prize. "Who do you love more?" The internalized message is, "Danny did it the best, so he is better."

The way parents treat siblings can set the pattern for how children relate outside of the family unit. Within this unit we learn morals, attitudes, ethics, and competitive social values. It is how the parent deals with the competitive rivalry between siblings that determines how effectively they get along with each other and in the outside world.

Always praise your children for their individual traits. Teach them to respect their differences. Teach them to share, resolve differences, and communicate with one another. If they compete, then it should be done in the spirit of a game— for fun—and not for your approval or disapproval.

When parents demand only excellence from their children, this pressure creates competition. A demand for excellence is good as long as it is based on individual and not collective capabilities. Collective capabilities, in families, demand all children succeed at a certain level, and compete with one another in order to stimulate the drive to accomplish. Look at the family of Joe Kennedy. John, Robert, and Ted were high-achieving, ambitious children who grew up to work in the most competitive arena—politics. Each child was groomed for a life in public service. Joe Kennedy set up a competition between his sons—choosing the one he felt would succeed in a run for the presidency of the United States. Many members of the Kennedy clan have acted out in rebellious and violent ways in order to get attention from their family. There have been drug charges and philandering. In such a high-achieving arena, it is hard to get noticed, and children may act out negatively. This is not unusual— many families set up competition among their members as a way to push the stronger children to the surface, often at the expense of the weaker ones. Parents who do this may be expecting all their children to achieve equally well in all areas. But each child is an individual with different strengths and talents.

Generational Messages

The critical parent never lets the child "win." Parental disapproval can be a subtle criticism—"Why did you do it that way?" "You never try hard enough," or "If I were you, I would have . . ." These messages stay with us throughout life and can influence the way we behave with our own children. Many adults still seek the approval of their parents and are plagued by the feeling that they can never fulfill their parents' expectations.

The generational influence from childhood is strong. The disapproving parent feels angry perhaps because he was emotionally abandoned and criticized in childhood. According to psychologist Dr. Jill Model Barth, "The wish to belong and fit in are usually parents' projections of their own fear of rejection and abandonment." As Dr. Barth explains, "This calls into question the function children provide for some parents: narcissistic expressions of themselves." If a child does not live up to the narcissistic expression, then the parent criticizes. Criticism is a type of control. A parent who pushes through criticism is fearful of losing love from his child. He controls to maintain the child's dependence. But eventually the child will rebel out of anger, and the parent will be emotionally abandoned again, replaying his childhood trauma.

A Parent's Own Early Pain

Most of us begin the parenting process with positive and loving intentions, but the pain of whatever early childhood trauma, disapproval, anger, or criticism we ourselves endured can intrude. The early development of a child is a complex interactive process. The child is shaped by her environment (nature) and the parents' interaction with her (nurture). The way you respond to your child in part is determined by how you were responded to. Were you yelled at? Criticized? Bullied? Pushed past your limits? It is vital to come to terms with your own early pain so you will not repeat negative emotional patterns with your children.

Early pain sets the groundwork for how we parent. If issues are left unresolved, they can have unforeseen negative effects on your child. We tend to parent much like our parents and their parents before them. If there is poor bonding and unhealthy interactions, this can carry over from one generation to the next. When Nathan was a child, he was willing to do anything to please his father—but could not succeed. Nathan learned quickly that if he displayed any anger or negative feelings around his father, he was punished. So Nathan started having temper tantrums: he was willing to get negative attention simply to connect with his father. His only outlets for his stifled feelings were at school and on the playing field. At one point he was expelled for hitting a boy with a baseball. His father pulled away from Nathan further. This early imprint was very powerful. Nathan repeated this pattern when he became an adult and punished his own son, Josh, for expressing angry feelings.

Not until we deal with unresolved issues can we break the conditioned bonds of generational patterned behavior. These patterns are what cause us to push our children too far too fast without being cognizant of their needs. And the cycle only stops with your awareness of the past and of how you were influenced by parental approval or disapproval. This understanding of your life helps you as a parent because it can clarify areas that cause you to push your child.

Amy could never please her mother. Each accomplishment was always met with the attitude that she could do better. If she got all A's and a B on her report card, her mother focused on the B. If she made a sports team, her mother dreamed of her being the star player. If she looked pretty, her mother talked about the girls who were prettier. Now a successful businesswoman, Amy is driven by her need to constantly "prove" that she is good enough. As a mother, she is always pushing her son to practice piano and study harder so he can make the honor roll. Amy could never succeed in her mother's eyes, and now her son will always fall short in her own eyes.

Subtle or overt parental criticism erodes self-esteem. A child goes through life as a driven pleaser, but never pleases himself. His ego is tied to someone else's perception of himself. This psychodynamic can cause anxiety, social dysfunction, and depression. The lack of self-esteem can actually lead to more serious problems like eating disorders and chemical dependency.

Ironically, parents can actually "kill" their competitive children's spirit by criticism. The child starts to question her abilities, and eventually she doesn't believe in herself. The internal message is, "If my parents tell me I'm not very smart, I must not be." But these messages can be turned around with awareness and willingness. Is it easy to change? Absolutely not. Conditioning is strong.

Modeling is the strongest of all personality imprinting. Often one parent has a stronger impact on a child's behavior than the other. Imprinting begins in infancy when a baby copies the parents' facial expressions and responds to them. If you cry, the baby is disturbed. If you smile, the baby will feel calm. It is common to see a little girl copying how her mother dresses, styles her hair, and puts on her makeup. Some boys will model masculine traits in their fathers and act boisterous or loud. This gender modeling or gender identification is what sets the stage for psychological modeling, which has a more profound impact on your child. Psychological modeling determines how your child will behave. If you are aggressive and withholding, the child will see these traits as acceptable. The boy whose father loses his temper on the tennis court will probably grow up to lose his temper. An alcoholic parent will often have children who become alcoholics. The negative pattern of modeling continues.

The patterns of behavior we establish in our lives are deeply rooted. But I assure you that changing negative patterns can be one of the most loving things you can do for your child.

The following is only a beginning. The roots of generational conditioning are complex. How we push our children to the edge and why will be further explored throughout the book.

Breaking Free of Patterns

- Try to find out what influenced your own parents. How were they disciplined? Were their parents competitive? Pushy?

- Don't be too hard on yourself. You are trying to become a better parent. You cannot hold on to self-anger if you want to move on positively.

- Define what you want to change. For instance: "I want to stop being critical of my child every time she gets a grade lower than an A."

- Let things go. Do not focus on every negative aspect of your behavior or your child's. Be willing to give up certain issues.

- Don't be defensive.

- Be aware of your actions for two weeks. Chart how many times you display positive and negative behavior toward your child. Awareness of negative patterns will allow you to break these same patterns by seeing what areas you want to change and how often you repeat the behaviors.

The Unconscious Self

After identifying parental patterns, it is important to be aware of negative messages we send to our children through our "unconscious self." These messages form part of our child's ego. The unconscious self also reflects the world around us and thus functions in the world in a particular way—aggressive, possessive, overly competitive, manipulative, honest, trustworhy. If a parent is not clear as to what human traits are important, then his child may be equally confused.

There is faulty thinking in the concept that if you excel at something, you are either a superior human or a better person. Some parents unconsciously instill in their child the idea that if you are good at something (sports, arts, academics), then *you are good*. The child may come to believe that his talents or genetics are what make him a good person. But without the human tools for success, being a good athlete or the top student is a shallow goal. This is a difficult concept to grasp, especially in light of today's faulty heroes.

For instance, athletes, who were once revered for their kindness, good deeds, and compassion, now make headlines for spousal abuse, drug charges, and beating up coaches and referees. These competitive gladiators are the people your children look up to. In films and video games, the tough guy is the one children admire, whether he's nominally the hero or the villain of the piece. These are some of the role models that have been accepted by our society. Yet parents complain about their children's aggression and anger. If we as a society push children to compete and we place in their paths inappropriate role models, then we cannot expect them to be perfect citizens.

Many will disagree with this view. Some argue that it is

important to be a successful professional—life is expensive, and it takes push, guts, and know-how in order to get ahead. They pose the question, "What's wrong with being competitive if it helps my child get ahead in life?" Ask yourself these questions:

- Is it more important that my child be highly accomplished or a good person?

- If my child isn't number one, will his life be less meaningful?

- If my child doesn't meet my expectations, do I think I am less?

- Is my child a reflection of me? Am I a reflection of my child?

- Do I interfere too much in my child's life? Am I controlling or concerned?

Most parents are quick to declare, "I love my child unconditionally," but it is the unconscious self within the parent that gives off negative messages to his children. It is the comparisons to others, the unhappy looks on our faces, the subtle comments, our body language, and sometimes displays of overt disapproval that lead children to feel diminished. It is essential that parents make themselves aware of any negative messages their unconscious self may be sending their child. These behaviors must be changed, along with any overtly negative ones, for a child's self-confidence to thrive.

Building Positive Messages

In order to help our children, we need to build positive messages that they can internalize, as well as teach our children self-control and problem-solving skills. Negative statements will not motivate a child. Parents may use negative statements without being fully cognizant, and their child starts to believe something is wrong with her.

In order to build confidence in your child so she can succeed on her own, without fear of criticism, it is necessary to support her choices and feelings. This is often difficult for the competitive parent who is devastated if his child opts not to play a sport or go to dance lessons. There is a fine line between teaching and guiding your child and controlling her behavior. The controlling parent does not trust his child's choices. He is psychologically afraid that if his child stops competing, she'll somehow fall behind all the other children. But the opposite is true. Children who are allowed to use their natural curiosity will be more creative, interested, and successful because they are exploring freely without the fear of making mistakes. They will learn from natural consequences and put up less resistance to parental controls.

Building positive messages is one of the most important tools in guiding our children and creating high self-esteem. Our job is to act as a support system without constantly sending judgments.

The following chart gives positive statements a parent can use to redirect negative critical behavior.

NEGATIVE STATEMENT	POSITIVE STATEMENT
Why can't you kick the ball harder?	You kicked the ball really well in the last half of the game.
You shouldn't feel that way.	I'm sorry you're feeling angry.
You'll never pass math. You're a lousy student.	You must feel pretty bad about your math grade. How can I help you?
Sue is such a better artist than you. Why can't you draw like her?	You and Sue have different styles of drawing. Both are interesting.
You look terrible in that dress. It's too short. Take it off.	I like your taste in clothes. Is such a short dress appropriate for this school function?

Now, fill in the chart on Parent Patterns. Make a check every time you make a positive and negative comment. The positive comments should outweigh the negative, and eventually you want to go for no negative feedback.

PARENT PATTERN CHART

	WEEK 1		WEEK 2	
	Positive	Negative	Positive	Negative
MONDAY				
TUESDAY				
WEDNESDAY				
THURSDAY				
FRIDAY				
SATURDAY				
SUNDAY				

How we were parented and pushed to compete creates the framework for how we treat our children. Unless we stop the cycle of negative parenting, our children are destined to suffer the consequences. Awareness is the beginning. In the succeeding chapters, you will explore the process of parental pushing and learn ways to break the negative cycle, reorganize your priorities, and build healthy internal structures. You cannot change the past, but you can alter the future. You can bring up early pain, work through your feelings, and turn negative interactions into positive loving ones.

If you focus on becoming an outstanding human being—which is truly the best—then you stand a far better chance at success for both yourself and your child.

3

MAKING THE GRADE

Fourteen-year-old John couldn't "make the grade." He was a C student, and he believed his prospects for the future were dim. His parents were beside themselves with concern. They hired expensive full-time tutors and sent John to all sorts of enrichment classes, to no avail. Every test came back marked C, which meant average, and average was not good enough for John's parents. They felt that in the high-charged competitive world of academics, you had to get all A's to succeed. They constantly pushed him to study harder and do better. They tried to be encouraging, telling John that they knew he had it in him to be at the top of his class—he just had to work harder. John, who was usually a happy child, began to feel unworthy of his parents' expectations. He saw himself as stupid, a failure who would never amount to anything. He stopped studying. Why bother? He just kept frustrating his parents—and himself. If he didn't try, no one would be disappointed.

This push for grades hurts the parent-child relationship because the parent places more emphasis on the grade instead of the relationship. The ultimate judgmental mark on a report card can have an enormous impact on the way a parent views his child and ultimately on the way a child views himself. If a child falls short of parental expectations, the parent may see him as not being good enough—smart enough.

Kids tell me constantly of their fear of not making the grade and the overwhelming pressure to be a good student. One mother recently told me about her twins, a boy and a girl. The boy, she said, was a genius. But because the girl had slight dyslexia, the mother hoped she would marry rich. Her children were in kindergarten.

The way you approach your child regarding his intellectual abilities can greatly affect his life far into the future. Children are vulnerable to whatever information parents communicate to them over time. If you constantly tell your child he is not smart, he assuredly will begin to view himself as intellectually inept and act accordingly. If you reaffirm your child's intellectual prowess and let him know you have faith in his abilities, he will try to do his best.

But for many of us, "his best" is not good enough. A child's "best" may not be the goal of his parents. The parent who pushes wants his child to be the best among others, the top of his class, the star athlete. What if his best means he can't compete on the level that you expect?

What if your child gets a D or even an F? Does that mean *he* is not good enough? Does this signal he will not be happy, fulfilled, or even successful? Or does it mean that you, the parent, don't feel you're good enough? This is an important point to explore. Remember, grades can be a weak barometer of success. There are thousands of stories of men and women who reached the highest pinnacles of success in their fields, yet struggled in school. Albert Einstein is a good start. He barely passed math. Churchill and Rockefeller were poor students. Bill Gates did not finish college and never cared for school very much either. Some skeptics may say these are exceptions. But are they? Can you think of some successful people who didn't go to college?

The competition race for entrance into private schools has left entire families devastated by a rejection slip not offering a young child a place in a prestigious school. Parents spend hours and hours filling out applications, asking friends of friends to get well-known people to write recommendations, offering to donate money to a school, and sending their child to tutors in order to prepare him for admissions testing. Some mothers put their unborn child's name on the waiting lists for "Ivy League" preschools. How do you interview an infant for nursery school?

Sally and Barry took their three-year-old daughter, Lynne, to a private school in New York for an interview. The parents expected that little Lynne would be well behaved and compliant. They desperately wanted her to be accepted into the school. After all, all of their friends' children were attending school there. After a nerve-racking parents' interview, Lynne came into the room, threw off her shoes, and started to suck her toes. Her mother was aghast. The headmaster shook his head as if to say, "No way in a snowstorm is this toe-sucking kid getting into our school."

When Lynne got her first rejection slip, she was outside happily playing with her Barbie dolls. Sally and Barry took the rejection personally. If only they had bought bigger shoes for Lynne, her feet wouldn't have hurt, and she wouldn't have sucked her toes. If only they had been wealthier, they could have donated a building, and Lynne could have sucked her toes all day and night.

The bottom line here is that it was Sally and Barry who felt the competitive social pressure to send Lynne to a private school—Lynne herself was perfectly happy and did extremely well in the neighborhood preschool her parents finally agreed upon.

The parents who push to get their child into high-pressured schools are not taking into account a child's strengths and weaknesses. Some schools are a poor fit for some children. Your child may not perform well in a highly competitive environment. He may do better in a creative school or perhaps a school that offers different tracts, ones suited to his capabilities. Many schools are strictly test oriented—that is, all the learning is fact based, geared to passing an exam. There is no other measure of how much your child is learning. For poor test takers, this style of learning is counterproductive. Why put your child in an environment where he has to compete with children who learn only one way and are lauded because they test well?

Academics is not the only area of success. A psychologist friend once remarked to me about my then young daughter, who was struggling with her grades, "Your daughter may never be an honor student, but she will grow up to be a magnificent adult because she has so many amazing qualities and life skills." I have held on to those words for many years as my child approaches adulthood. Life is the ultimate journey, not the few years your child is in school. Yes, grades are a measure—but not the only one. If school comes easy for your child, that's wonderful. But if he struggles, don't push him into a box with other children. Let him be free to find his own wings.

Each of us approaches the world differently, based on a particular learning style. Psychologist Howard Gardner writes in his book *Frames of Mind* that there are seven types of intelligence. In each person one type dominates over the other six. This influence shapes a person's perceptions and determines how one learns best. Ultimately, this affects the formation of the individual's personality.

Seven Types of Intelligence

- *Linguistic* learners like words and languages. They like to read and write.

- *Logical* learners enjoy sequencing ideas and are good at mathematical relationships. They are highly organized and generally good at standardized testing.

- *Spatial* learners are creative, with good memories. They are artistic and inventive and often like architectural tasks.

- *Bodily-kinesthetic* learners are athletic and physical. They use instinct more than logic and may excel in theater.

- *Musical* learners recognize rhythm, pitch, meter, and tone.

- *Interpersonal* learners are gregarious people with good social skills. They communicate well and are usually good at public speaking and oral assignments.

- *Intrapersonal* learners understand their emotions. They are more serious, focused, and introspective. They work well independently.

Can you identify your dominant style? Your child's? Problems occur when your child's dominant trait clashes with your own. Adam is linguistic. He reads voraciously and adores language. He is an intrapersonal man who is serious and calm. His son, Alex, is a bodily-kinesthetic learner. He can't sit still for long and does not enjoy reading. He is interpersonal and learns by listening, doing, and communicating. He'd rather be playing sports and spending time with friends. Adam sees Alex as "wasting time"; he thinks Alex's sociability is frivolous. Their relationship is stressed because Adam can't see the possibility of Alex's becoming successful if he does not "buckle down" and become more studious. But in truth, Alex just approaches life differently than Adam. Alex is on student council and plays intramural sports. His talents and learning styles are different from his father's. They are not good or bad—just different.

It is important to respect who your child is and not attempt to change his nature. Trying to make a shy child gregarious or a musical child a star athlete can ultimately break his spirit. You cannot remake what is the essence of your child. You *can* socialize him, expose him to new experiences, help him mature, to learn, to bring out his best qualities, but you cannot change his basic personality. All children have their own academic styles. It is vitally important to assess your child's learning style and adapt his academic success to it.

If you don't respect learning differences, then your view of competition will turn into intolerance. You might think, "If only I could change a few things in my child, he would be perfect." But perfection is a standard that does not exist in the real world. Respecting—even embracing—your child's differences is the first step toward positive parenting.

Overidentification

Parents who overidentify with a child, that is, take on the child's life and relive their experiences through him, can cause great harm, especially to a child with a fragile ego. A child might work hard in the beginning to make a parent happy, but true success can only be sustained when the desire and effort are internal.

Rona, fourteen, was a poor student. She had learning differences and attention deficit hyperactivity disorder (ADHD). She struggled to get good grades but could not live up to her parents' expectations. Her mother was a bright student who quit college to marry and have children. She felt she didn't live up to her potential and go to medical school as she'd always dreamed. Now she was tortured that Rona would never be able to become the student or doctor she wished she had been. The tension to achieve almost led Rona to a breakdown. Rona was especially poor in math and science, subjects her mother had always excelled in. Because of the push for grades, Rona's mom failed to see any of Rona's other good qualities. She was disappointed and kept thinking Rona wasn't trying hard enough. Rona became so discouraged, she didn't bother to study. If she could not meet her parents' expectations, then why try? The effect her mother was trying to achieve was counterproductive—and ironically Rona became an even poorer student, adding to the heightened tensions. Rona's mom had dreams for herself that she didn't achieve. She wanted her daughter to fulfill them, so she could live vicariously through her child. But Rona was her own person with her own strengths. Her mother needed to find ways to help Rona minimize or overcome her challenges, and to understand who her daughter is and to encourage the traits that make her an individual.

Use the following chart to think about your best qualities and your child's best qualities. Then consider the obstacles that hold both of you back from appreciating yourself, and your child. Instead of making comparisons to your child, work on your own personal obstacles—nurture the positive characteristics and make changes to those that get in the way of your relationship with your child. Look for parallels between you and your child. Where you notice differences, think about how to nurture, not change, them. As for obstacles, redirect negative behavior by awareness and positive reinforcement.

WHO IS YOUR CHILD?	WHO ARE YOU?
What are your child's five best qualities?	What are your five best qualities?
1. _____	1. _____
2. _____	2. _____
3. _____	3. _____
4. _____	4. _____
5. _____	5. _____
What are the five biggest obstacles that hold your child back?	What are the five biggest obstacles that hold you back?
1. _____	1. _____
2. _____	2. _____
3. _____	3. _____
4. _____	4. _____
5. _____	5. _____

Homework Traps

Ten-year-old Ali was not all that interested in school. She was a happy girl who got by, and her teachers adored her. When her work started looking too perfect, her teachers confronted Ali. It was clear that the reports and papers were being done by someone other than Ali. When asked, Ali broke down in tears. She confessed that she begged her mom to stay out of her schoolwork, but she refused. Ali's mom was so involved that she constantly criticized Ali's work. Eventually, Ali let her mother do her work rather than argue. Ali lost her motivation, believing she could never satisfy her mom's standards.

When it came time to take class tests, Ali was unprepared because she had no investment in the material. The homework became her mom's. The work became her mom's. When she got A's, her mom was pleased. But the A's gave Ali no sense of accomplishment. After all, she hadn't really earned them; her mom had. Eventually, Ali and her mom were called in to see the teacher. Ali's A was changed to a C, and her mother was asked to leave Ali to do her own work.

Every parent wants her child to do well. But the line has to be drawn between "helping" with homework and "doing" your child's work. Janice Hubbard, an expert in teaching study skills to students, believes that "daily, detailed involvement by parents is the surest predictor of a child's academic success." According to Hubbard, this factor has more impact than tutors, computers, or teacher aides. If you start working with your child at a young age, certainly by first grade, by the time she becomes a teenager, she should successfully be able to manage on her own the homework load.

Hubbard does not believe that a child's notebook is private property (although a teen's is) and says it is essential that you see to it that your child's homework assignments are completed. This establishes good work habits for high school and college. If a child is resistant to your help, then give her a chance to work alone, but periodically check to make sure the work is complete and correct. Most younger children will welcome input, since it is a chance to spend time with her parent.

Although Hubbard thinks teens need more privacy, if a teen is doing poorly in school, then all bets are off, and a parent has the responsibility to monitor the teenager's work (with or without complaints). The parent should look over each assignment and test and help *guide* the child through the homework—not do it for him.

It is the competitive parent that can't stand to see the homework or research papers less than perfect. Part of the reason for homework is to allow your child to make mistakes so he can learn. If you do his work, his projects, his research papers, you are robbing him of his chance to build internal self-motivation.

Superstudents

For some children, academic competition spurs them on. They are what I call "superstudents." They are fueled by grades and relish seeing all A's on their report cards. But for this type of student, the competitive internal push can also cause psychological and physical problems.

Fifteen-year-old Jamie was so nervous before tests, he would break out in hives all over his body. If a child is so frightened that he will somehow be a failure if he doesn't get better grades than his peers, then he will not want to even try, for fear of losing.

Superstudents are driven, and thus spend an inordinate amount of their time studying. These kids are so overly focused on academic grades that they may not pursue outside activities: sports, art, theater, music. Many do not socialize and, therefore, are shunned by kids in school. They are developing only one aspect of their personality. One ten-year-old girl said her mother enrolled her in S.A.T. classes even though she wouldn't be taking the college entrance test for six or seven more years. The girl gladly went to the classes believing that they would give her an edge over other students. She wanted to get a perfect score.

Superstudents place such a high expectation on themselves that anything short of an A sends them into a depression. The school counselor couldn't convince one sixteen-year-old boy that a B on his report card would not prevent him from going to a good college. But for this boy, that B represented failure of a sort, and this affected his self-esteem.

Then there is the student who is so worried about not measuring up that he will go to any lengths to ensure a good grade. This includes cheating, buying tests and papers off of the Internet, and paying someone to write a report for you or do your homework.

Aron was told that if he didn't get at least a B in chemistry, he could never get into a University of California school. He panicked. Desperate, Aron found someone to sneak out a copy of the final. He paid the thief one hundred dollars. Although this type of behavior is not new in history, it certainly is more prevalent today.

The problem begins when schools keep pushing the requirements higher and higher. Most college-bound high schoolers are required to take four years of a language, chemistry, physics, calculus, and at least three advanced placement or honors classes. Probably three-quarters of the previous generation wouldn't have gotten into college because they couldn't have passed some of the rigorous class requirements. What happens to the average kids who want and have every right to go to college? They are being pushed down—relegated to a "less than" status. Are we becoming a country of exclusivity—only encouraging the top 2 percent? This type of society produces superhuman robots, not humans. People are varied and interesting. Diversity is what creates a culturally rich society. We need artists, athletes, thinkers, and dreamers along with scientists and doctors.

The Bully Competitor

The bully. This type of child competitor is willing to hurt and humiliate in order to win. The bully is so afraid of not being on top that he will threaten, push around, and insult others to secure his position of top dog. Parents who push a child to "do what it takes" to win, who encourage their child to use physical threats, cheating, and intimidation, are helping to foster bully behavior.

Children bully because it gives them a sense of power. That power makes them feel superior. But in reality the bully has low self-esteem, and his fear of failure drives him to pick on others. Kids who feel good about themselves don't have to bully anyone, because they know who they are and accept their strengths and weaknesses. Their parents have managed to instill the idea that they are okay—they are good enough. Unfortunately, competition has become aggressive. There are higher incidents of bullying in our schools. Children who feel so insecure about their abilities that they have to resort to bullying in order to be successful are ultimately doomed to social isolation.

It is not unusual that a bully child will have a bully parent. The bully parent so overidentifies with his child that he cannot separate his drive to win from his child's. Bully parents smother their children, demanding perfection. If the child does not win—or perform to the parents' requests—such parents will often withdraw love.

If you suspect that your child might be displaying bully competitor behavior, it is important to be aware of the following points:

- Look at your own behavior. Are you pushing too hard for a win? Are you aggressive and disrespectful?

- Tell your child you love and accept him whether he wins or loses—and show him you mean it!

- If you see your child acting like a bully, discipline him immediately.

Bully behavior should never be tolerated in children or adults. We live in a world where cooperation, respect, and tolerance will make you a real winner.

Child Empowerment

Empowering a child to reach his or her *own* potential—not one that is unattainable—should be your ultimate goal. That is the purpose of assessing learning style, personality, and strengths, and of setting goals. But if you want to give your child empowerment, you have to begin by taking the power out of your hands and putting it into his. When a child takes personal responsibility for his work, he begins to own his pride. He is not just studying for you, but for himself. If he makes poor choices, then he will have natural consequences: a poor grade, feeling badly. If the parent owns the feeling, then the child has no investment in the outcome. His attitude is, "My parents say only an A is acceptable, they push and yell at me constantly—they do the homework! Why should I bother?"

One mother was aghast that her child only got a C on a research paper. The mother had done most of the work and exclaimed, "How dare that teacher only give me a C?" Her child had no power, no ownership of her grades.

There is a difference between motivation and a competitive dictatorship. When your child does not display the same desire for academic success that you do, it is incumbent on the parent to try to motivate his child or leave him alone. It is destructive to constantly badger your child and make unrealistic demands on him. Every child works at his own pace. Because your friend's child is already mastering algebra in seventh grade, it doesn't mean your child has to. But there are motivational techniques that can help stimulate and bring out the best in an oppositional or understimulated child.

Learning can be contagious. It can be an amazing adventure as long as you are respectful of your child's learning style. If you are passionate about classical music, play CDs at home. Take your child to a kids' concert. If he loves animals, take outings to the zoo. Go on nature hikes. Pick leaves and spot birds. "Life" is a wonderful school. Not everything is taught in a classroom, and not all intelligence is measured by grades. Hands-on learning can be the most enriching for children and spark a serious interest.

If you dictate that your child follow in your footsteps, it is almost sure to backfire. It is important that a child's choice is truly *his* choice, and to choose, he needs to be exposed to as many things as possible to choose from. But do not sign him up for dozens of classes. Do expose him to music, art, sports, science, nature—and books, books, books. Go together to the library often. If your child is a reluctant reader, perhaps rethink your choice of subjects. A story about wizards is unlikely to motivate a child who wants to know about volcanoes. Enlist the help of your librarian. Read to your child daily.

Most importantly, your child shouldn't think that learning is something done separately from day-to-day life. All the things you normally do together can be an implicit learning experience. Cooking together can become a subtle math lesson in weights and measures. Raking leaves can become a nature lesson. Even dropping something on the floor can become a science lesson on the nature of gravity! These activities will begin to stimulate the learning process. But remember, in your zeal to teach new things to your child, if you force your child and push too much information on him, you are defeating the purpose. Not everything you do should be a lesson. Some children will never like math or science. Some will dislike writing. But by connecting some aspect of these subjects to real life, you help put random facts in context. Your goal is to motivate your child to become a self-learner and embrace life as an adventure—not a race.

It should be noted that the spirit of competition—perseverance, self-confidence, and hard work—is not negative. Standing alone, these traits can help form the basis of positive learning techniques. It is the degree to which we persevere that changes our outlook on things. The idea of winning at all costs is what impedes personal growth.

There is the argument that "winning" is all that counts, that life is based on who wins, comes in first, and who is victorious. Yet someone will always be the loser in a competition. It is how he loses that is important. Look at Apolo Anton Ohno, American Olympic speed skater in the 2002 Winter Olympics. He was just a few feet from the finish line and a gold medal when he went down, edged out by another skater. Although he didn't come in first, he was gracious, humble, and mature. He said that he was fine with a silver medal because he'd skated his best. He was confident in his performance because it wasn't about the medal, but personal fulfillment. Apolo is a winner.

We all want our children to be winners. Now here's the challenge. In order for your child to feel empowered and to want to compete, it may be necessary to pull back. American parents are by nature protective, competitive, and driven to ensure that their children do better, get more, and have more opportunities. There are ways to empower your child to become responsible and to care about learning. The following list will help you to motivate without pushing.

- Take time to find out who your child is, what are his likes and dislikes, personal style and strengths, and then empower him to make decisions by using his personal learning style. Encourage a bodily-kinesthetic learner to think about sports, a spatial learner to explore art.

- For younger children, start off by offering choices. Do you want cereal A or B? Do you want to wear stripes or checks? Do you want to read a book about bears or elephants?

- With an older child, instead of threatening or bribing a resistant child to study, encourage her with her *own* power. Say, "This is *your* schoolwork and your life. You must make the decision as to what is important."

- A teen especially will be less rebellious and angry if you give him confidence in his abilities. If the child or teen is still resistant, then he alone pays the consequences, i.e., a poor grade. Let him make mistakes and empower him to take responsibility for his life.

- Lastly, empower your child to love learning, not the goal of getting into a good college. This is accomplished by role modeling. Keep books and music in your home. Go to museums and concerts. Have family discussions with older children about current events. Go on nature walks and to science centers. Make learning new things a natural part of their world.

Goal Setting

For many parents, reality can be intolerable. Some children will never be academic competitors. Many may have school difficulties. Approaching your child with remarks like, "Everyone gets better grades than you," and "You'll never get into college," can have a long-term devastating effect. Not only will it exacerbate a problem, but these negative statements will further antagonize your child and cause him to pull away from any suggestions you make.

Some kids with learning problems, who have competitive

parents and siblings, feel lost. Their attitude is, "Why bother studying, I'll never be as smart as my friends or siblings." A child may crave attention, even if it is negative, and a bad grade will certainly get Mom and Dad to sit up and take notice.

It is more important to be supportive and goal-oriented than to be grade-oriented. First you need to identify the problem, then help your child define her goal. It is vital that your child define the goal for herself. For instance, don't say, "Denise, you want to get A's in school." Ask Denise what her goal might be. Perhaps she just wants to get a better grade on her next test. Your *child's goals* can be simple: to move her grade up one notch even if it's from a D to a C, to get all her homework in on time, or to get a positive report for good behavior for a week. Your *parent goal* is to get your child to take responsibility for her actions. If she owns her problems, then she feels she must—and can—take steps to solve them.

Once she has defined the goal, try to help her think of solutions. Keep her proactive in the process rather than reactive. You will be pushing if you take over the problem-solving process and treat it as *your* personal problem. If you do, then your child will not take responsibility for her actions, and she won't find motivation to make changes.

You can ask her for suggestions for her personal solutions. She might ask for a tutor for extra help, a class on time management, or help setting up a more efficient plan to study at home. You can ask your child if she would like your suggestions. Ask questions. "Do you take notes when the teacher gives out assignments?" "Do you understand what the teacher is talking about?" Now you might be able to set up a study program to help your child. You can even work together if your child wants to. These techniques will teach your child to set goals and become her own advocate.

Praise and Encouragement

The critical parent will not have a successful child. If you want your child to feel empowered to achieve, be encouraging. Encouragement helps to create a positive relationship in the family, which in turn translates to other areas of your child's life. Encouragement helps your child develop self-confidence and self-reliance. It's about encouragement, not necessarily praise. Praise is what a child receives from outward sources—grades, trophies, or others' opinions about him. There is a stark difference between praise and encouragement.

Some parents overpraise everything their child does. He becomes overconfident, and, therefore, when he does not succeed at something, he is shaken and may fall apart. He has no inner resources to draw from.

Encouragement builds self-esteem, one's inner confidence

and the feeling that "I'm okay." These feelings emanate from unconditional self-acceptance and self-respect. You cannot *give* your child self-esteem. But you can perpetuate it by your behavior. This means temper your criticism, increase cooperation, and help your child develop self-reliance.

A child develops self-reliance when he feels that his world is a safe place, that his parents have faith in his ability to solve problems, and that he is capable "as is." Your job is to let your child make mistakes—even fail—so that he can rebound and develop a sense of self. Many children are afraid to take on new tasks because they are so used to their parents criticizing or judging the outcome.

Helping your child to appreciate his good qualities and not dwell on perceived shortcomings can instill good self-worth. Teaching him to put his talents to good use can also perpetuate feelings of usefulness. Self-confidence does not come from what others think about you. It comes from what you think about yourself, and that is why encouragement as opposed to praise helps to perpetuate self-esteem.

The chart on the next page delineates the difference between praise and encouragement.

In order to compete on any level, one must feel confident in one's own abilities. A child never feels "good enough" no matter how he performs on a test or task if the parent keeps raising the bar and says, "Next time you can do even bet-

PRAISE	ENCOURAGEMENT
Can perpetuate a child's viewing himself from another's perspective.	Focuses on the child assessing his own accomplishments.
Is assessed by grades, rewards, and trophies.	Helps a child accept his efforts and develop a desire to learn without rewards attached.
Can lead to a child blaming others when he fails at something because the expectations on him are so high.	Helps a child become willing to make mistakes and start again—ultimately, to take responsibility for himself.

ter." When your expectations are so high, your child may give up because there is too much pressure.

By recognizing and encouraging what is special and wonderful in your child, you will be helping him to grow into a psychologically healthy person. Acceptance and unconditional love set the foundation for your child to know courage and confidence when facing challenges, academic or otherwise, in his life.

4

THE SPORTS PUSH

Who's Really Kicking the Ball?

Allison had been playing soccer since she was six years old. Her father, Seth, pushed her into working with a private coach at an exorbitant seventy-five dollars an hour. He made her try out for a club team and go to soccer camp during her vacations. The fun went out of soccer for Allison. But Seth lived and breathed soccer. It was *his* passion, but no longer Allison's. When she told her dad that she wanted to quit, Seth was enraged. He would not hear of it. He took it personally, as if Allison were trying to hurt him.

"This is my dream," he implored Allison. "This is your

ticket into college, and I won't let anything get in our way." Allison became more and more resentful of her father's interference. During one game, he pushed one of the referees. He was ordered off the field and banned from coming to her games. Allison was horrified. After seven years of playing, she finally quit. She was so turned off to soccer that she never returned to the sport, and her relationship with her father remained damaged.

Part of the problem with kids, parents, and sports is determining "who is really kicking the ball." When parents become overly invested in their child's experience, they take what should be a fun learning experience away and infuse it with adult actions and emotions. A child's fragile self-esteem can be hurt. If you doubt this, watch the parents on the sidelines of any children's Saturday baseball, soccer, football, or hockey game. Observe parents screaming and tearing their hair out. "Run faster, kick harder. Why can't you score? Why can't you get a goal?" The perplexed child wonders, "What's wrong with me? I'm trying my best." If parents and coaches constantly question a child's sports ability, motivation, and talent, he begins to have no self-worth. He believes that his coach, his parents, and his teammates are mad at him because he isn't good enough. Children learn by trial and error. That is what childhood is about. They need to make mistakes so they can improve.

Many parents are not tolerant of mistakes on the field or

in the gym. They lose sight of the importance of teamwork, good sportsmanship, and the fun of playing. The basic tenets of sports are lost because parents become overly involved. They view themselves as the winner or loser, and the push for their child to be the best player puts an enormous burden on the child. The parental ego, if not checked, can be a destructive force. The playing field becomes a battleground instead of a place of learning and growth.

In Jupiter, Florida, parents were behaving so badly on the sidelines that in 1999 Jeff Leslie, head of the Jupiter Tequesta Athletic Association, was compelled to give classes in parental ethics on the soccer field. The parents' jeering and yelling at players and referees—and the fights that broke out—had reached an intolerable level. Leslie, dismayed at the parents' behavior, said, "Parents were screaming at their kids after the games. Some intimidated opposing players on the field in an effort to mentally unhinge them."

A group of soccer girls who were interviewed on the news revealed that they no longer enjoyed playing. One girl was devastated when her dad lost his temper. She felt that the parents were using their kids to compete with each other. These parents encouraged their children to do whatever necessary to the other players in order to win; this included being vicious, knocking down other players, tripping players, and pushing them.

The ultimate horror happened in Boston when one father

beat another father to death at their children's hockey practice. The argument that led to the beating was simply over one child being given more playing time than the other. There is a sense of elitism and egotism associated with sports these days. Kids and parents use calculated aggression aimed not just at winning, but at demonstrating power, exploiting weakness in others, and instilling fear. The biggest fear that people have is failure, and a parent who overidentifies with his child transfers the child's perceived failure onto himself. The parent cannot see this as a learning experience. Rather, he views a loss in sports as his personal failure. Parents need to question their own motives and expectations in regard to their child's participation in sports.

Winning has become too tied to who we are. The "we" is not our children, it is us. A survey showed that 95 percent of youth players were more interested in having fun than in winning. Children need a sense of freedom and the choice to play or not play a sport. This is part of the process of growth. A child's emotional growth is based on his ability to make choices and then learn from any mistakes that arise from his choices. When a parent intercedes in this process, the child feels insecure, uncertain of his actions. The child may question his abilities. How can he learn that he is capable if his parent always runs in to save him? In previous generations, kids were told to fight their own battles—to work out their problems. Few parents would have picked a fight with a coach or an administrator to give their child an edge. Overcoming obstacles was considered a good way to build character.

The Price of Glory

For those parents who are determined to push their child into sports believing that it will be worth the physical and emotional risks, there is a price to be paid. It's important to understand what's at stake and how to make thoughtful parental decisions.

Billions of dollars per year are spent by competitive sports schools and other institutions on top-level young athletes. This kind of money draws the best coaches and players who see college scholarships and even professional play as the result of their efforts. At the intense levels of some of these teams, coaches don't accept excuses for missing practices or games. They put sports before family functions and school finals. One might justify this kind of commitment if the end result were that coveted scholarship. But the statistics show that few succeed in this compared to the thousands who aspire to a scholarship. A mere 2 percent of kids receive them.

Brian remembers his father pushing him very hard in baseball. "If I was hurting, he told me to play through it. He'd yell at me not to be a wimp. I ended up with a bum arm and a lousy relationship with my dad, and for what? I didn't even get a scholarship. I let my grades go to hell because of baseball, and I didn't get into any good colleges."

Dr. Shane M. Murphy, a sports psychologist, writes in his book *The Cheers and the Tears* about how competitive sports can lead to children being bullied by coaches, injured by overtraining, and rejected if they can't achieve increasingly difficult goals. Children are treated like professionals in high-stakes arenas where the pressure is relentless. Often coaches, so intent on winning, push children so hard that they break down. Some kids have a thicker skin, but others who are more vulnerable can be damaged psychologically by an overly ambitious coach. Therefore, it is up to the parents to navigate around this and make thoughtful decisions about how far and how fast to let a coach push their child.

The worst case occurs when a child is marginally talented but the parent cannot accept this fact. Somehow that child "pays a price" for being an average athlete. There is no enjoyment in sports—only the agony of not being good enough in his parents' eyes. This is a tremendous burden on a child who feels he is letting down his family, his coach, and his school.

Some parents will delay needed surgery so their child can continue to play without taking time out for the procedure and a long recuperation period. Dr. Bert Mandelbaum, a leading Los Angeles orthopedic surgeon specializing in sports injuries and the doctor for the World Cup soccer teams, laments that more and more young athletes are arriving at his office with injuries he previously saw only among much older players. Some children are required to perform like professional athletes. Kids do not have the stamina and training to keep up the furious pace of sports today. They are overtrained and often play with injuries before they have fully recovered.

"Kids as young as nine and ten are coming in with ligament injuries, stress fractures, and torn tendons," says Dr. Mandelbaum. "Young girls are especially susceptible to injury because they are not building up the necessary muscles to support the high level of play, especially on the soccer field."

Younger children may be in danger of bones growing improperly if they are pushed to practice too rigorously. The end result may be a permanent injury or disability. The U.S. Consumer Product Safety Commission and the National Youth Sports Safety Foundation estimate child athletic injuries and costs nationwide have had more than a 650 percent increase in 2001, the most in seventeen years.

Besides the damage to the parent-child relationship and physical injury, kids pay another big price: losing the love of the sport. The passion of play goes out of kids. The need to win becomes too serious. Sports are no longer fun.

A parent's role is to give love and support unconditionally, regardless of a child's performance. The relationship deteriorates when it is based on a child winning. The pushy parent becomes a coach, constantly lecturing, arguing, and instructing the child. When a parent pushes a young athlete too hard, the child can suffer physical injury, but the parent-child relationship will most certainly be injured. If a child has to wear a knee brace at age ten, he can become depressed. But when his parent rejects him because he's not playing hard or well enough, he can be devastated.

Yet, there are those who take the opposing viewpoint, arguing that a child must train incessantly and stay visible in order to attract the attention of the top recruiters. On some level, this may be true, but when a parent starts overtraining a seven-year-old, something is bound to break down—the child, the parent, or both.

If a child does have talent, then it should be assessed properly. The child should be trained by a knowledgeable coach or trainer—someone who understands the differences between a child's and an adult's physiology.

What to Look For in a Coach

Coaches often become surrogate parent figures for children. A good coach will model positive values: sportsmanship, fairness, tolerance, persistence, determination, discipline, honesty, and humility. This may sound like an ideal, and indeed no person is perfect, but you should try to find a coach who attempts to teach these rules of honor. Sports are a wonderful microcosm in which your child can learn about the world. If his coach emphasizes winning at all costs, doing what it takes at the expense of others, and success tied only to winning, these are the values your child will take with him into the adult world.

The following are guidelines for what to look for in a coach:

- The person should understand the sport and children. He or she does not have to excel at the sport personally, but should have a competent knowledge of the fundamentals.

- The coach should understand a child's physical development and what girls and boys are capable of achieving at a certain age.

- The coach should be attuned to personality differences. Some kids can be pushed harder than others. Some children are highly sensitive, cry easily, and need a gentler approach. Others let the pressure roll off their backs and don't take the tough approach to heart.

- The coach should be a motivator—a person who tries to motivate with positive as opposed to negative input. For instance, instead of pointing out every mistake, the coach should reinforce what the child does correctly.

- The coach should be sensitive to cultural, physical, and racial differences in children. One coach I know of used racial differences to emphasize a child's basketball talent. This was inappropriate and insensitive.

- A good coach will instill a sense of conduct that builds on the ideas of fair play, effort, cooperation, and striving for excellence. A coach should not argue with referees or other coaches, use profanity, criticize players, allow cheating, or make kids feel they are worthy only if they win. If winning is the sole goal, then you should rethink if this is the kind of environment you want your child to be in.

It is better not to coach your own child. A parent is too emotionally enmeshed to be unbiased. He will be either too hard or too easy on his own child; it is difficult to treat your own the same as his teammates. This puts enormous pressure on both the child and the parent.

The Ideal

Children, especially adolescents, are extremely impressionable. They are prone to being sensitive to comments, and they want to get parental approval. They take things seriously. When parents set up an expectation, in this case becoming the best athlete, the child tries to meet the parental ideal. The parents project their longings onto their child, who works to please them. The child may push his own needs and feelings aside. Unconsciously, the child lives in fear of not meeting the parental ideals. Subconsciously he worries he will be rejected by his parents. He thinks, "If I'm not good enough, I'm not lovable." The child might not be aware of these thoughts, but these powerful messages will drive his behavior and affect his self-esteem.

This was the case of Diane. At six, she was taken by her parents to a gymnastics class. Diane showed some genuine talent and she loved the sport. Her parents enrolled her in gymnastic classes, and Diane successfully competed on a regional level. The better she got, the more she trained. She began a rigorous gymnastics schedule—getting up at five A.M. to practice before school and practicing on weekends.

When Diane became a young teen, her body changed, and the petite, agile gymnast grew taller and bustier. Her mother, who had hopes of Diane making it to the Olympics, put her on a strict diet. But this could not change nature. Because of her mother's obsessions, Diane absorbed her mother's concern for her body. She believed something was wrong with her. The more she grew, the more obsessed with her body size she became. And she was devastated that no matter what she did, she couldn't make her mother happy. Her changing body no longer fit the "gymnastic body ideal" or her mother's. So she punished herself. She turned the anger and hurt inward, and she became anorexic. She couldn't live up to the ideal so she went to the other end of the spectrum. She became so frail and weak that Diane could no longer even consider gymnastics. Diane had to be admitted into a hospital when her eating disorder got out of control. She never fully recovered and her weight became the prime issue in her life.

It is important to examine your own motives and to understand why you want your child to participate in sports. Many parents want their children to be a better or more successful version of themselves. Do you see sports as a way to improve your child's emotional and physical development? Do you want your child to be successful so you can be proud of him? Do you want your child to be more like you?

Appreciate your child for who she is. Take pride in her unique talents and personality traits and let her know she is special. If your child shows interest in a sport you like or excel in—great. Mentor and encourage her. But make sure you let her enjoy herself and help her keep competition healthy and the activity fun.

Sports are a healthy outlet for children if approached positively—by this I mean if parents encourage athletic participation as a fun, relaxed way to get exercise, experience teamwork, and learn new skills. But if parents become overly competitive and involved and put pressure on their children, then sports can turn into a negative experience. According to Dr. Jenn Berman, a sports psychologist and eating disorder specialist, "When parents push too hard, they create anxious, depressed children. Parents rob their children of the chance to establish inner discipline, which is important for long-term success."

A parent often equates his personal success with his child's winning or losing. This pressure on a child can be overwhelming. In essence, the parent is making his child feel responsible for him. The parent, whose own ego is not fully developed, fails to separate himself emotionally from his child. Instead of a sports loss being an opportunity for growth and enjoyment for the child, it becomes a source of validation for the parent. Each victory is felt as a success for the parent, while a loss leaves him feeling unworthy, rejected, a failure. This dynamic alters the parent-child relationship. The child tries to feed the parent's self-esteem and soothe it with each disappointment. This is quite a heavy responsibility for a child.

Parents often invest their vicarious desires in their children. It is wonderful to take pride in and enjoy your child's accomplishments, but as Berman explains, "You can't control the ultimate score. What you can do is change your attitude. How you accept a win or a loss will help move your child forward towards focusing on *his* personal best."

Gender Bias

Parents have been known to foster negative behavior by encouraging a child to see his teammates as "the enemy." This is especially prevalent with boys. One father set up a competition between his son and another forward on his son's soccer team. The father argued with the coach, telling him that the other forward on the team was a terrible player. He demanded more playing time for his son. This father put individual needs over those of the team. His son became a bully on the field, emulating his father's behavior.

The message boys are often given from early childhood is, "Winning is everything." There is an emphasis on sports as a way to communicate power and position in adolescence. Contemporary society doesn't value the intangible benefits of athletic accomplishment such as self-confidence and a strong, healthy body, but places the emphasis on fame and fortune. A male's identity is often wrapped up in his ability to win at sports. Being part of the team isn't enough. The competition for "first" is the goal, and the pressure to compete takes its toll. Part of the problem with this attitude is the failure to teach boys ways to communicate other than the use of physical strength.

There is a psychological link between sports and the development of self-esteem. According to Dr. Eric A. Margenau, author of *Sports Without Pressure,* when a child excels in sports, he is fulfilling the need for fantasy. The fantasy aspect is played out when boys watch sports on television and fantasize about being Shaquille O'Neal, Tiger Woods, or Pete Sampras. These fantasies are normal, except when parents put on the pressure and start making comparisons to professional athletes. The parent's fantasy is so wrapped up in his boy's sports success that he can't see beyond his own need for ego fulfillment.

This happened to Matthew, an avid sportsman and basketball player in high school and college. His son, Mark, showed little interest in sports. Matthew forced Mark to play basketball because "all the boys did." But Mark was not good at sports. He didn't like basketball. Matthew refused to accept this fact. Mark turned away from sports in favor of theater, and this eventually impacted his relationship with his father. He admitted that he felt inadequate as a male because he didn't like sports, and years later he went into therapy to work out these feelings and this anger toward his father. Mark felt guilty because he didn't measure up to his dad's expectations. He never felt good enough in his father's eyes. You can't force a child to like sports. You can—and should—respect what he does like, what he excels in.

There are certain prevalent expectations for girls in regard to sports as well. When I was growing up, the girls who were jocks were considered "unfeminine." Girls were expected to be cheerleaders. This was frustrating for girls who secretly longed to be part of a team. I had to wait twenty-five years before I finally realized that women could participate in sports—all sports.

Twelve-year-old Stacy was a terrific athlete and constantly

outshone her thirteen-year-old brother. In fact, she wanted to play Little League but was discouraged. Her dad held her back with his criticism, but he pushed her brother and encouraged him to play. Eventually Stacy gave up sports. As an adult, Stacy had trouble with any type of competition. She was not confident in her abilities. She was especially intimidated by men and found it difficult to compete on any level with a man. She was caught in the traditional, macho view of girls in sports and this carried over into other realms.

Fortunately, sports are no longer considered "unfeminine." Girls will readily play "boys' sports." Conversely, boys who are not big, tough football or basketball players have found gender acceptance in tennis, golf, swimming, and gymnastics. (But they are not as comfortable taking dance lessons or being cheerleaders.) The sports stereotypes have somewhat diminished, but in their place, especially among girls, is a killer competitive ethic which, as we've seen, can have unhealthy repercussions regardless of gender. There needs to be a balance between the emotional, psychological, and physical aspects of raising sports-minded boys and girls.

Destructive and Constructive Competition

There are two types of competition. *Destructive competition* involves a person trying to eliminate his opponent and destroy him. Destructive competition is based on a narcissistic premise that winning at all costs is the end goal. But this type of athlete is driven not only to win but to outshine other teammates. He sees his participation not as a team member, but as an individual. Oftentimes, these players do not last because they are unable to be good team members and actually get in the way of play. You probably have seen these athletes: the soccer player who doesn't pass the ball; the football player who won't throw to the quarterback; the basketball player who dribbles and holds the ball too long. These players are so interested in winning "their point" that the team is in danger of losing the game.

When parents push their child to be "the star," they foster destructive competition. They put so much emphasis on the child's performance that they may create ruthless bullies on the playing field. Not only that, they are likely to push their child *away* from the sport. When a child has to work too hard to perform, the rewards of winning are outweighed by pressure to win.

Destructive competition needs to be outgrown if a child is to mature and learn to be a fair and decent human being as well as an athlete. It can be replaced by constructive competition. *Constructive competition* advocates using the opponent to get inspired rather than seeing the opponent as the enemy. Constructive competition emphasizes the child doing the best he is capable of, rather than advocating that the child destroy the opponent. Constructive competition fosters a love of the sport, and a respect for coaches and fellow teammates.

When constructive competition comes into play, children are able to enjoy many benefits in athletics:

- Experiencing peer approval

- Identifying positively with a group or team

- Achieving goals as part of a team

- Sharing a common experience

- Increasing self-confidence

At His Own Pace

The ability to accomplish a feat at his own pace reinforces a child's emotional development. Never say to a young child, "That's wrong," or "You're doing that poorly." The *doing* is what is important. This is especially true with young children, who learn from success, not failure. This brings up the idea of putting younger children into a sport before they are ready. A child who is not developed physically or mentally may not be able to tackle a sport that demands a certain amount of strength and mental conditioning.

T-ball can be too demanding for toddlers who are asked

to stand still, wait for the ball, react, and remember the rules. Soccer calls on children's natural skills of running and kicking. But any organized sport should not be played before a child is old enough to have the cognitive understanding of what is being asked of him (usually around age five or six). Also, experts agree that young people function better in programs where game scores and league standings are not kept. In this atmosphere, competition, hostility, conflict, and disappointment are minimized. A child can learn the game and the rules and refine his skills. When the fundamentals are mastered, and he is much older, competition becomes part of the game. But at this point, the child is committed to the love of the sport and not focused on beating his opponent. It is a parent's job to direct his younger child away from the final score and work on mastery and skills. It is the doing in itself that is important. Sports help your child stay fit and make new friends.

Even if a child loses or comes in last, perhaps he has bettered his time or kicked or thrown the ball better. See these steps as an accomplishment. Small gains should be seen as success. A sense of mastery can only come when the child is ready. You will know because your child will naturally move on to a new task. When a child is allowed to move at his own pace, he gets a sense of mastery at each level, and this can enhance the enjoyment of the sport.

The following do's and don'ts advocate constructive ways to cope with winning and losing at sports and helps parents guide their children in a positive, loving way.

Do's and Don'ts of Being a Good Sports Parent

- Do direct your child so that he helps others on his team to be successful. By being supportive, the child realizes he doesn't always have to be the top player.

- Do learn how to tolerate losing. Losing can be seen as a learning experience. What skills need to be worked on? How can you work together better as a team?

- Do model good sportsmanship. The way you act and react will show your child how to act. If you become aggressive and yell, chances are, so will he. Teach him to be a good winner *and* a good loser.

- Do listen to your child. If he tells you, "I don't want to play," do not force him.

- Don't analyze the game. You are not a sports announcer. Let the child make mistakes, thereby learning from these mistakes.

- Don't yell at your child or other players. Kids have fragile egos. Come to the games with a positive attitude. The sports experience is the child's—not yours.

- Don't be a sideline coach. Your child has a coach. If you disagree with his leadership, talk to him privately, and respectfully, off the field.

- Don't compare. Your child's ability should not be judged or rated vis-à-vis that of his teammates.

Examine your own motives for wanting your child to play sports. Ask yourself:

- "Do I want my child to play because I was good at sports, and I want him to be like me?"

- "Do I want my child to be a better athlete than me?"

- "Do I want my child to be like all the other kids?"

- "Do I want my child to develop physically and mentally?"

- "Do I want my child to be the best?"

Siblings and Sports

Siblings can become especially competitive in sports. Parents often inadvertently encourage this rivalry. Or one child will have a passion for sports, while the other has no interest. In order for the parents to treat their children equally and downplay sibling rivalry in sports, *Sports Illustrated* for kids has some valuable guidelines for parents to follow:

- Do encourage all your children to try new activities and not limit them to your choices.

- Do offer praise for whatever your children do.

- Do allow your children to pick their own sports, regardless of what sports their siblings choose.

- Do praise siblings for teaching and supporting one another.

- Do give equal attention to nonsports interests.

- Don't play favorites.

- Don't compare your children.

- Don't limit your children's areas of interest.

- Don't forget to encourage younger siblings and girls.

- Don't let your younger child become just a spectator.

- Don't encourage competitive behavior beween siblings.

The Sports-Obsessed Child

There are some children whose own inner competitive drive is stronger than their parents' push for sports success. These children are "sports obsessed." They push themselves too hard, are never satisfied, and find little joy in other activities.

Because these children are so enmeshed in their sport, it is up to the parent to help his child create an identity other than "Joey the football player" or "Annie the soccer player." Children who are too sports obsessed can injure themselves or burn out mentally.

A parent needs to set boundaries:

- Limit practice time.

- Encourage your child to take on another activity (art, community service, computers).

- Take a team approach and refocus on the efforts of the whole as opposed to the sole performance of one.

- Communicate. Share your concerns with your child. This conveys love and refocuses family priorities.

- Validate other areas of your child's life. Is he helpful at home? Does she help out with siblings? Is he a good student?

A parent who is secure and competent will not push a child into a situation in which he clearly feels uncomfortable. Parents think they know what's best for their children. But in truth, children intuitively know what they like and dislike from an early age. Sports can be an incredible learning experience for children. Sports are healthy outlets that teach coordination, socialization, self-discipline. In sports, children have the opportunity to break through limits, something that will help them deal with tough times in their adult lives. Children can learn to bounce back from a loss, appreciate a victory, and develop friendships. Parents should nurture a child and appreciate and encourage life skills: kindness, generosity to teammates, honesty, and truthfulness. These are "talents" that will make your child a superstar forever.

5

BEAUTY AND THE BEAST

What Is Beauty?

Our world is focused on the way we look. From the time you are a child you are aware of who is overweight, buck-toothed, cute, and gawky. You see images on television, in movies, and in magazines. There is an emphasis on the way we are physically perceived. You see that you can get others to notice you because of the way you look. How strong is the image of the good-looking, popular girls and boys burned in your memory? Did you see visual images that you knew you could never live up to? Or perhaps you were one of those who escaped social ostracism because of your looks. Do you fantasize about your child looking a certain way? And if she or he doesn't, how does that make you feel?

Every culture defines beauty in a subjective way. In Thailand, if you have a large bridge nose, you are considered attractive. In China, the whiter your skin, the more beautiful you are thought to be. In some countries, if you are heavier, you are more desirable. Why are the standards of beauty so diverse? One may argue that standards of beauty are determined by what is most rare in that culture. In a poor region where food is scarce, an ample woman is seen as special, privileged. In a country where conditions force many to work outside in the hot sun, one with pale skin would be viewed as elite.

But America is a melting pot; countless cultures are represented. So what is beauty here? By and large, the standard is set at something most people can't achieve. Flawless size 0 models with large breasts grace our magazines. The truth is, not even they live up to the ideal of beauty. Plastic surgery, starvation, and an army of handlers create their image. And when this too fails to produce perfection, there is always airbrushing.

Why do we give such high regard to beauty when it isn't real? Worse yet, even if someone does possess beauty, it doesn't last. Inevitably looks fade and all that remains is the inward beauty of the human being.

Issues of beauty can plague young people. The societal message they receive is, "If I am good-looking, I will be successful." Children ask, "Am I pretty? Handsome? Thin? Do I have a nice nose, lips, hair, eyes?" Teens devour magazines wondering why they don't look like the waif models. My daughter had freckles as a child. She thought if she scrubbed hard enough, she could erase them. Somewhere she got the message that freckles were not okay.

Twelve-year-old Alicia was panicked when her normally developing body sprouted breasts and hips. Then, when she got her period, her face broke out and the girl was inconsolable. She felt betrayed by what was "normal." Her mother, Sara, tried to explain that the images she saw in magazines were controlled by retouching, and the looks she coveted were more art than life. But Alicia continued to obsess about what she perceived as an imperfect face and body.

When she went into therapy, Alicia revealed that she heard her mother always complaining about her wrinkles, her imperfect nose, her fat body. Her mom pored over beauty magazines and commented about the way the women looked. Sara was taken aback when the therapist explained that Alicia was modeling her behavior. Sara's beauty values were focused outwardly not inwardly. Her daughter was emulating much of the behavior she saw at home as well as in society.

The drive to compete for the "beauty brass ring" is futile. Athletics and academics require skills and brainy endeavors, but the race for who's prettiest is shallow. That is not to say that looking healthy and fit, well groomed, and stylish are not enjoyable and admired by many. Beauty has its place as a sidebar, not the main feature. But society places so much pressure on a child to look a certain way. It is like saying, "You must be prettier than everyone else or you are ugly." It is difficult enough for some children to go through developmental changes, especially adolescence, without feeling geeky. These are the times to tell your child how lovely and wonderful she is, especially when her mirror may be telling her otherwise.

Inner Messages

The competition to be prettier or more handsome or more popular can create an anxious, self-conscious child who has distorted images about her physical features and self-worth. She may have unrealistic visions of who she is and why she is valued.

Children tend to internalize the messages that they hear, see, and listen to. These inner messages come by way of parents, peers, and the media. Some of these messages are:

- "It's a shame, but you really do have your father's nose."

- "Are you going to wear that?"

- "Don't eat sweets. You'll get fat."

- "Your skin is breaking out!"

- "Your hair is so thin—like my mom's."

Society hits us harder with images of tall, impossibly thin supermodels and airbrushed ads of "perfect" people selling thousands of products that promise to make us look better. The message always is, "You don't measure up, so you need to use our toothpaste, hair shampoo, diet pills, clothes, makeup, etc., in order to be okay."

One of the most dangerous inner messages young girls get today is to flaunt their sexuality in order to be popular. The ethos of boys phoning for a date, girls demanding respect, and young people waiting until marriage or at least a serious relationship to have sex has all but disappeared from our society.

The gender competition starts to heat up when boys and girls realize they are different and the competition extends to one's own sex. Girls vie to show up the next little girl by displaying prettier clothes and more Barbie dolls. Boys battle over physical talents like who is the better athlete or who has the most trucks.

Parents tend to further push competition when kids reach adolescence by stressing that girls need to look pretty "for a boy" because her competitors are other girls who may look better. The messages girls receive—even if not directly—are often body-oriented, like it's good to have "big breasts" or "thin bodies." Boys get messages about being "tall" and "muscular." Many kids who can't compete on the level of looks use sexuality to prove desirability and attention. This tactic invariably harms reputations and self-esteem, and can have serious health consequences—for example, AIDS, other sexually transmitted diseases, and unwanted pregnancy. The consequences of this behavior are long-lasting, often causing further problems as this conduct and mindset are carried into adulthood.

Tom, always told what a great-looking guy he was, is now in his twenties. He was encouraged as an adolescent to compete to "get" the most girls, and as he grew older, he spent so much time conquering one young woman after another that he was never able to find a loving, bonded relationship. He saw every woman as a conquest. He boasted about his many women but secretly admitted that he was lonely and tired of the constant competition.

Some parents are even encouraging their daughters to be the aggressors with boys. This often sends mixed messages to boys who back away from these girls because they feel confused by not having to compete. Girls are now told it's okay to be sexually competitive.

When parents are overly concerned about their children being popular, they may be too permissive. After all, they don't want their child to be ostracized or left behind. But by not saying "No," parents give the unspoken message that sexual behavior is okay.

After interviewing hundreds of parents, I found that few believed that their child was sexually aware. But the pre-teens I talked with were quick to say that everyone was sexually advanced. This sexual behavior at a young age is due to the way in which society exposes us to sexual material. Young people watch television, which exposes them to a constant bombardment of sexual images: MTV, *Howard Stern, Sex and the City*, soap operas. Some of these shows may be entertaining, but they are not appropriate for young people. They can overstimulate young teens. They present sex and nudity as perfectly acceptable. Therefore, in order to be accepted, kids emulate what they see on television. Hey, if their heroes are doing it, no big deal, right?

The problem lies with a parent who so badly wants her child to be popular that she indulges the child in this fantasy. The child is allowed to go to any party (even unsupervised ones) and dress seductively. There is unspoken approval—as long as her child is accepted into the right group, the parent doesn't interfere.

Simply stated, the problem is there is not enough *disapproval*. Today's parents are afraid to say, "No," "Not okay," "Don't even think of it." These messages need to be integrated into a child's psyche. The push for "pretty" and "popular" can lead to permissiveness, which puts kids on dangerous ground, being exposed to too much at too young an age. They feel shaky and often frightened, being forced to deal with things they are not mature enough to handle. The desire to be part of a group can lead a child to make poor decisions, some of which can lead to lifelong consequences. You may need to reassess your beauty priorities and help your child embrace what is really important.

The following list can help you begin.

REASSESSING BEAUTY PRIORITIES

- Do not emphasize how people look, especially your child.

- Focus on internal characteristics—intelligence, a sense of humor, kindness, generosity, humility.

- Be realistic about the media. Explain the manipulation of looks by airbrushing, computers, lighting, photography, etc.

- Never point out what you perceive as negative traits—a big nose, squinty eyes, obesity.

- Discuss childhood physical changes as normal and natural.

- Suggest reading material that has a hero or heroine with whom your child can identify.

- Look at your own motivations. Are you obsessed with your looks and how others perceive you?

- Inspect your child's reading, video, and theatrical material. Don't be afraid to say "No" to what you deem inappropriate information on dress, makeup, diets, or oversexualized images.

How Eating Disorders Begin

When Lara was a young girl, her mother's mantra was, "Be thin, be pretty, be popular." If she had these ingredients, her mother assured her, she would live a happy life. So Lara, who loved her mother, began to work hard to be the thinnest, prettiest, most popular girl in school. She had almost achieved her goal, but then she entered high school, and there were thinner, prettier, more popular girls. Lara thought, "How can I be happy if I'm just like everyone else?" She decided to get thinner than her competition. She stopped eating and lost thirty pounds. She was a "bag of bones." Lara was once again the thinnest girl in school. She was happy. She then went to work on being the prettiest. She dyed her hair blonde and got her nose "fixed," her teeth bleached, her breasts enlarged, her skin lasered, her eyebrows arched. She was looking quite pretty. Her mother gave her parties that cost a small fortune, and all the kids came and danced the night away. Lara was now very popular, and everyone wanted to come to the parties.

One day, a new girl came to school. She was thinner than Lara. Her cheeks were more chiseled, and her father was one of the wealthiest men in town. Lara became depressed; she couldn't compete. She started to eat candy bars to mask her depression. She gained fifty pounds. Then her dad lost his job, so they couldn't give expensive parties any longer. Lara wasn't so popular now. Because she was so unhappy, she stopped caring about her looks and she was mean and grouchy all the time.

Lara was especially angry at her mother. Why had she told Lara that all she had to do was be thin, pretty, and popular? Lara hadn't developed an interest in anything else. So now she just sat around all day eating candy bars and crying. Lara gained more and more weight. She realized that she no longer had to compete: people felt sorry for her, and she got a lot of attention. She liked this. One day, she went to school and there was a new girl who came to school, but she was fatter than Lara. . . .

This fable tells an important story about competition and our cultural obsession with how we look. It also points out that there will always be someone thinner and prettier, and emphasis should be on one's personality (the inner package) more than one's looks (the outer one).

According to researchers, 50 percent of nine-year-old

girls and 80 percent of ten-year-old girls have been on a diet. Mary Pipher notes in *Reviving Ophelia* that 50 percent of teenage girls are on a diet, and 20 percent of young women have an eating disorder. Although these statistics may sound alarming, they are on the rise among younger and younger girls as well as boys.

How did this competition for the perfect body get so out of hand? Did it start with the body image of Barbie or Hollywood's food-starved actresses? Fashion models since the turn of the century have become thinner. The advertising and clothing industries have perpetuated the use of underweight men and women to show off more skin.

The problem with present-day society's view of eating disorders, specifically anorexia, is that instead of reviling the disorder, many young women and even adults envy the thin people and view them as having willpower and control. And it's not just thinness that is coveted. It is the striving for perfection—the tightest buns, the flattest abs, the buffed chests and arms. No one is satisfied with himself. Our desire to sculpt, reshape, diet, and exercise our bodies into some idealized image has become an obsession.

Although much is written about young people and eating disorders, there is not an awareness of the competition tied to body image. Perpetuated by the media, virtually every magazine features either impossibly thin or muscle-bound sculpted models idealized as perfection. It would be difficult for any young person not to compare him- or herself to these models, and almost everyone always falls short of the ideal.

Marissa, only ten, was sitting in a diner with her mom, her friend Nicole, and Nicole's mother. Marissa, a healthy girl of normal weight, ordered a hamburger and French fries. When Nicole, healthy and similar in size to Marissa, ordered the same, Nicole's mother canceled the order. She told the waitress to bring her daughter a salad with no dressing.

"You'll gain weight eating *that* food."

Suddenly, Marissa's mother looked panicked. *Should I cancel the order? Will Marissa get fat? Am I a bad mother? Am I fat?*

The confusion and obsession begins early in childhood when the first cookie is snatched out of a child's hand by a well-meaning parent who is concerned about her child's diet. Food, in many instances, becomes the enemy as children become adolescents. These young children once pranced around in their skin totally uninhibited, not aware that the world they inhabit would soon tell them that something was not quite right with their bodies. It may happen when a girl gets her period and everyone keeps telling her how much she is "filling out." She soon will equate "filling out" with being big. Or perhaps it's when a young boy's mother sighs as she drags him to the "husky" section of the department store.

Heather was a weight-loss fanatic. She was on a perpetual

diet, counting calories, keeping a food journal, never letting a fat gram enter her mouth. She exercised incessantly and became depressed if she wasn't the thinnest of all of her friends. Heather became so obsessed with her weight that she was unable to concentrate on anything else. She compared herself to celebrities and rock stars in magazines and was convinced that everyone else was thinner. When Heather stared in the mirror, she saw an overweight person. Kids at school made fun of fat girls, and Heather would rather die than be fat.

Heather decided that the only way to compete with the other girls was to stop eating. If she didn't eat, she wouldn't be fat. So that summer Heather gave up food. She lost twenty pounds. She never got her period or developed normally. Her bones became weak, and she couldn't concentrate due to headaches and dizzy spells. By twelve, Heather, by now a very unhappy girl, was diagnosed with anorexia nervosa. Was it the years of obsessing over the scale? Or was it the result of a culture that creates cookie-free images of men and women who are so thin that no normal person can measure up?

Mothers worry about their children's (mostly daughters') weight to the point of obsession. Their mind-set seems to be, "If my child is 'thin,' she will be more popular, successful, and happy." But parents need to redirect their messages. For instance, the word "thin" should be replaced with "healthy."

And body size and shape should never be equated with success or happiness.

No mother wants her young daughter to have an eating disorder, yet many anxious mothers have the very eating disorders they want to help their child avoid. Grown women are just as prone to the societal pressure to be thin.

My teenage daugher, who is an athlete, has a strong, beautiful body. Yet whenever I would see her binge on pizza, chips, and cake, I would get crazed. I would visualize her as becoming "fat." I worried that she would become out of control. This anxiety caused me to badger her about what she ate. I would say I only wanted her to eat healthy, but she knew my motives were to assure she stayed thin. I thought if she remained thin, her life would somehow be easier. This was faulty thinking on my part, and I knew it. Yet, I still worried about my little girl gaining weight.

Dr. Jenn Berman set me straight. She explained that I was the one feeling internally out of control. I was transferring my anxiety onto my daughter, projecting onto her my own childhood reality. I was a chubby child who became anorexic as a teenager. I starved myself down to 109 pounds and then I began to model. All of my self-esteem became wrapped up in my external looks. Yet, inwardly I still felt like that chubby little girl. I was now transferring my obsession with thinness onto my own daughter, who really was extremely different from me. She is an athletic, confident, happy child. I was damaging her self-esteem because of my fears of her not being able to compete with the skinny images in fashion magazines. But thankfully, she was strong enough to be her own person. She knows how lovely she is. She perceives her true self.

Although I am not proud of my actions, I share this story to serve as a lesson to other mothers. Although I am lucky that my daughter was—and remains—strong enough to resist my influence, there are many young girls who are not so strong. A young person's ego is extremely fragile. They are malleable beings whose sense of self is just being formed. Preteen girls are especially vulnerable to negative comments about their looks. They hang on your every word; they hear what appears to be a benign comment about candy having empty calories and think you are criticizing them.

Be careful of the messages you are sending to your children and be vigilant so that you can detect and react appropriately to any destructive beliefs she may have about her weight.

Do you recognize your child in the following:

- More than half of eighth-grade girls have dieted at least once this year, and 41 percent have dieted twice. Does this apply?

- Does your child always call herself fat or disgusting even though her body is normal?

- More than half of girls in school perceive themselves as overweight and are actively trying to lose weight. Does your daughter fit into this category?

- Does your child hide food? refuse to sit down at meals? sneak into the refrigerator late at night?

Signs of an eating disorder can show up in puberty. Be alert to changes in your child's eating habits or attitudes about her body. These are some typical signs (adapted from the *Baltimore Sun*):

- refusing typical family meals

- skipping lunch at school

- making continual comments about being fat

- being reluctant to shop for clothes because she gained a few pounds and doesn't want to look in the mirror

- hoarding food and candy (suggesting secret bingeing)

- withdrawing from friends

- exhibiting prolonged irritability and depression

Although eating disorders and body obsessions occur primarily in girls, boys are not immune. All the warning signs apply to boys as well as girls.

If you want to help your child with weight and eating issues, pull back. As a parent you need to de-emphasize food and body size. Your goal should be to help your child view food in a positive and emotionally detached way. If you follow these tips, your child will be healthy in body and spirit.

Food Issue Tips

- Serve well-balanced, healthy meals. If you take care of your body, so will your child.

- Discourage the idea that a particular diet or body size leads to happiness or fulfillment.

- Don't use food as a reward or punishment. It sets up food as a weapon for control.

- Don't constantly criticize your own shape by saying, "I'm too fat. I've got to lose weight," in front of your child. Such comments imply that appearance is more important than character.

- Body shape is genetic and out of your control, so don't push your child to be something he or she is not.

- Don't equate food with positive or negative behavior. The dieting parent who says she was "good" today because she didn't eat much implies that avoiding food is good behavior.

Distortion

Our children are a physical reflection of us. If what she sees in her child doesn't reflect back the best image of her, a parent may act disappointed in her child. Many mothers are willing to go to any lengths to help their daughters attain what is perceived to be beauty. The rise in plastic surgery among teenagers is staggering.

Young girls *and* boys are dyeing their hair, getting colored contact lenses, getting manicured, pedicured, waxed, plucked, massaged, zapped, pampered, and spoiled. But it goes beyond cosmetics. According to a number of plastic surgeons, more young girls are having nose jobs at sixteen, breast augmentation at eighteen, liposuction and laser surgery at twenty-one. These procedures were once reserved for older, wealthy matrons. Today, a middle-class mother will go into debt in order to give her child plastic surgery. It has become an accepted norm in our society.

Prized Beauty

The beauty pageant circuit for children has become a competitive training ground that can rob children of a normal childhood. Girls, especially, become adultlike dolls on display, being paraded around and judged on how pretty they are. What about the kids who don't get chosen by the judges? Do they feel like failures at five years old? Is the message to these children, "You aren't pretty or talented enough, so you lose?" This is not the message that young children should get. Young children should be playing, getting dirty, and feeling carefree. They shouldn't be wearing pink lipstick, mascara, and eyeliner, false teeth to cover gaps, and bouffant sprayed hairdos and showing off thousand-dollar sequinned party gowns. The entire meaning of childhood is lost on kids who are treated like lifesize dolls. Children need to learn their own lessons from the natural consequences of growing up and interacting with other children, not by talking and performing in front of a panel of adult judges.

One pageant mother said, "I want my child to be aware that there's always going to be somebody better than her. It's a hard thing to learn—it was for me—and I want her to start early."

This mother is using "better" to mean "look better," when the emphasis should be on how her child behaves as a person—her kindness, generosity, gregariousness, and spirit. This mom wants to work out her childhood pain through her daughter's experience.

Parents have bought into the myth that their children can do and be anything they set their minds to. But the reality is that we cannot compete in every arena no matter how hard we try because every human being has different talents, values, and drives. But some parents will push their children into a competitive area that the children wouldn't necessarily choose, because the parents value it. A mother might think, "I wasn't popular, but my daughter will be no matter what I have to buy or do for her." Some mothers push their children into beauty contests, spending untold amounts of money. Some contest veterans have admitted to spending close to ten thousand dollars a year to vie for beauty crowns. Many of these mothers take on two jobs in order to pay for entrance fees, dresses, and singing, dancing, and acting lessons. One mother said, "When my daughter wins, I'm that pretty girl."

To compete physically with others is a shallow goal. The quest for some unattainable perfectionism can lead to neurotic behavior because perfection is not possible. By emphasizing emotional, intellectual, and spiritual growth, a child will radiate beauty from within—a much healthier race to run.

6

SOCIAL COMPETITION

In Your Footsteps

We say we want our children to be humane, compassionate, and honest. But how do you live your life? You need to be aware that your child will model your social behavior and how you treat people. He will take on the values you expound. If you work insane hours for the purpose of making more and more money to buy the bigger house, the bigger car, and better "things," then your message to your child is that money is what is important, more important than even they are. That money takes precedence over people, over relationships.

Some parents will spend untold amounts of money on their child to impress friends and ensure popularity. When Carley turned eight, her parents gave her an elaborate birthday party complete with pony rides, a clown, a magician, and goody bags that were more expensive than most of Carley's gifts. Carley had few friends, but her parents invited fifty children. Carley's mom hoped this grand soiree would help her daughter secure friends. Only twenty-five children came and, to her parents' surprise and disappointment, the party did not help Carley become more popular. The other kids were turned off by Carley's bragging about all the things she had. Poor Carley—the message she received from her parents was that you could gain friends by impressing them with expensive things. Unfortunately, the children Carley went to school with just thought she was a braggart.

Carley's parents are not unique. We live in a society that's consumed with material things. People are often judged solely on where they live, the size of their house, or the car they drive. There certainly is nothing wrong with wanting nice things if you can afford them, but to judge a person's worth by their zip code or their financial assets is shallow and small-minded.

Some parents go so far as to choose their child's friends by their parents' financial status. They only want their child to associate with "a certain type of person." It doesn't matter if their child's playmates are smart, funny, or nice, as long as they're monetarily privileged.

But when we live by these standards, we diminish our own self-worth. When we spend so much time and energy competing to impress others, we surely set ourselves up for failure. The social bar can always be raised higher and higher by someone richer, better looking, and more prominent. Then what happens? Are we less when we can't compete on as high a level as previously? Of course not. But because of our skewed values, we cannot feel good about ourselves.

Still, many people work relentlessly to acquire things to keep up with the Joneses and impress the Smiths. They forsake relationships, time with their family, and sometimes their health to earn money so that they can acquire "things." They justify their actions by saying they are working so they can give their children "everything." But their children are missing out on some very important things: time with their parents and solid values on which to grow.

"Values," according to psychologist Terry Gopadze, "play a huge part in creating a good parent-child bond. Children learn early if they can trust their parents or not. If they don't have a trusting foundation, one that can be built on, then the child grows up feeling needy, abandoned, not good enough. Parents often replace time and attention with things. This inevitably creates a void in the child's life. The child then strives for things to fill up the void."

A child needs a model of social conscience and values. A child needs to know what ideals are important in order to make choices that will shape his life and view of the world. The pull of a society consumed with the obsession of money and social position is difficult to push up against; but parents can have a powerful influence by setting an example of a life that honors honesty, kindness, and compassion.

Love of Labels

We have become a culture of labels. They define our life because they signify acceptance—the ultimate competitive need. We are a group culture that thrives on others' approval. But what happens in the "striving for" is that you can lose sight of what you want and allow yourself to be defined by what others think you should have. If others define who you are, you can lose your sense of self. This is especially true of young people because their sense of self isn't even fully formed. If a child follows the group without being true to his beliefs, he becomes more interested in what others think of him, rather than discovering what he, himself, thinks. He will eventually grow into an adult who does not know what he wants or what can fulfill him.

Symbols are not reserved for the wealthy. No matter what

your socioeconomic level, there is always someone who wants to be at the top. They try to keep up with the right designer clothes, cars, computers, cell phones. Women will spend six hundred or even a thousand dollars on a purse with a certain insignia that immediately sends the message that it is expensive. Our society has gone into credit card debt to acquire things. Somehow things have come to define a person's character.

This striving for things filters down to our children, and advertisers know this. Just watch children's television and watch the commercials. Look at teen magazines featuring the latest glamorous pop star or hip, young actress. Children at a younger age are becoming aware of brand names and designer labels. Nike, Adidas, Puma, Royal are no longer just tennis shoes. Each shoe, depending on its cost and style, signifies how "cool" you are. Some parents will spend hundreds of dollars on sneakers for their kids. Gucci, Prada, Louis Vuitton are now hanging from the arms of preteen girls. Parents indulge child fantasies without regard to what these labels mean because, in truth, they want people to know they can buy their children expensive items. They justify giving kids cell phones, designer jeans, and leather jackets, believing they are just trying to help them fit in and feel good about themselves.

Somehow we believe that attaining the "right" material things and being part of the "right" group will boost our self-esteem. We equate symbols with success. But in truth, esteem is internal, not external. Validation that "I'm okay" must come from one's self. Self-esteem begins in childhood when we look to our parents for positive reinforcement, acceptance, and unconditional love. As we grow, we internalize that acceptance and develop self-love. An abundance of things can never replace a parent's love.

Inevitably what your child's friends value will influence him. Therefore, it is up to you, as the parents, to create a strong sense of what is important. The value of people should take precedence over things. A sense of responsibility to the community and to family is more important than a new "toy." Children need to know that designer labels go in and out of fashion, but human values will serve him well for his entire life.

Social Sport

Teams, social groups, and organizations can be positive vehicles for teaching your child about cooperation, loyalty, and friendship and the complexity of human interaction. Problems arise for kids when they are *excluded* from a social group. All kids want to belong, want to be accepted. Unfortunately, children can also be extremely cruel when developing exclusive subgroups. It starts as early as the playground when little Laine tells Jane that she can't play with her because Mary is Laine's best friend and they can only play together. As they get older, kids form secret clubs with secret handshakes. And it only gets worse when teens enter high school; high school is notorious for cliques and "cool" groups. The exclusivity is part of the fun, but it sure isn't fun when you are the one left out. Many of us can remember the feelings of not being part of "the" group. The exclusivity is often so fierce that some kids who are left out withdraw completely, while others lash out violently. One only has to mention Columbine to illustrate how terrible social competition can be.

While most cases are not so extreme, a child does first measure himself by how the peer group includes or excludes him. Ask any adult who was excluded from a group in school about his childhood and most likely you will hear an emotion-filled account. Some are still hurt, some are better, but the point is that these negative feelings have stayed with them all these years. And undoubtedly, the experience affected many choices they made in life.

Within the group there is often a hierarchy system. Some children want to set the standard and lead. They initiate the exclusion and decide who is "in" and "out." Many children can't feel good unless they make another child feel bad. This is usually a child who does not feel good about himself at all. Something is missing at the core of his personality and he needs to put down others in order to make himself feel good.

It is important to build social confidence in your children, to prevent them from excluding others and to protect them if they are the ones who happen to be left out. This will help your child feel successful as a person. He will rely on his own inner resources.

BUILDING SOCIAL CONFIDENCE

- Encourage extracurricular and/or after-school activities (orchestra, dance, drama) that put your child in a fun, enriching, and social situation.

- Help teach your child how to communicate effectively.

- Do not fight your child's battles.

- Do point out positive traits in people as well as your child.

- Do not emphasize how much money someone has.

- Use positive role modeling in your choice of friends.

Remind your child of his substance, not symbols that he has. Although social symbols can be fun, they are just that—fun. They can't make you laugh, think, reflect, or learn.

Those traits are gotten through deep friendships—a social tool that will serve your child well. By continuing to use the techniques to help boost your child's social confidence, not his social competition, he will be able to have a positive reflection of himself and attract friends.

Fifteen-year-old Patricia can't understand why she keeps losing friends. She is bright and attractive, and generally kids are drawn to her when they first meet her. But Patricia has a habit of always discussing how much money her family has and how many pairs of designer jeans she has and who is rich. She rarely describes a friend in terms of his kindness, intelligence, humor, or creativity. Her ex-friends say they dropped Patricia because she was "a competitive snob." Ironically, even though these kids came from wealthy, socially prominent families, they wanted to be liked and appreciated for who they were—not what they had. Patricia viewed money and status as a way to rise up the social ladder. But she couldn't attain what she desired because of a lack of internal substance.

My friend Jean was a man who helped people in developing countries better their circumstances by using their surroundings to create tools and what he calls "nature's machines." He lived a modest life with few material things. But his Sunday salons attracted the cream of London society. The people who attended did so for the stimulating people and conversation, certainly not for the water, tea, and crackers.

There was little room to sit, so most people sat on the stairs or on the floor. Jean and his wife, Catherine, were motivated by humaneness and, therefore, attracted people who had a need to bond with others in union, not in competition.

This clarifies for me the meaning of social health. In order to be successful, it is important to teach your child to be liked for who he is, not what he has. As cliché as this may sound, material things may fade away, but character endures and is invaluable.

Boys, Girls, and Bucks

The push for money has always been a particular emphasis for boys. How much money a man acquires has traditionally defined his status. The male ego is defined by dollars, not deeds. As society progressed, women took up the career path and created wealth, but females are still viewed by many as the "mothers," the nurturers, and so, on the whole, society's pressure on women to be wage earners is less than it is on men. But for a man, success is measured by the size of his salary. If a woman does work, she's not considered a failure if she earns less than her husband does.

Wealth forgives a multiple of "sins" for men. Less-than-attractive older men who have money often have young, beautiful women surrounding them. Sometimes the lack of personality is overlooked if the bankroll is big enough. We, as a society, have even excused bad behavior in wealthy men. Just think of Wall Street giants who go to prison for fraud, only to go on to have lucrative careers.

Young boys get the message about the value of money early on from their fathers. A disturbing example of this is exemplified by the Menendez brothers, who went on a spending spree after murdering their parents. The boys led a lavish lifestyle; their father gave them everything they wanted, but he was domineering and controlling. When they were children, Lyle and Erik were told what to eat, who to spend time with, what to read—even what to think. Their father was grooming them for success; he had reached the top through hard work and determination, but he wanted his sons to reach success in a more refined way. The pressure to please their father was intense, and the boys grew to resent it. The final straw came when their father threatened to disinherit them. The boys plotted to rid themselves of their father and in the process get his money. These boys were taught to value money above all else—even their father's life.

Another case is the Woodman brothers, who had their parents murdered. The motive centered around gambling and other debts the men had incurred. The brothers received the message from the time they were children that money was what was important in life. One brother, whom I knew as a teenager, said that his dad placed money above his family. When the brothers got into financial trouble, they had no internal ego resources to draw upon and saw no way out other than to have their parents murdered so they could inherit their fortune and pay their debts. This is a sad story with a tragic ending, but a sobering lesson in the message sent to boys about money.

If a boy grows up thinking his self-worth is determined by the size of his bank account, then he is being done a disservice. He will expend all his energy striving for financial success above all other things. His relationships will be at risk because he will never be sure if he is liked for himself. He will feel insecure. The value of money overshadows his value and his worth as a person.

Girls are also given messages about money, but often they are mixed messages. As more and more women enter the workforce and start earning significant salaries, they too join in the competitive race for promotions and salary increases. They are buying their own homes and cars and other symbols of success. But even as they're told they should earn more money and get more things, they are also fed the message that they can only respect a man who makes more money than they do. Many parents tell their daughters, "It's just as easy to marry a rich man as it is a poor man." Therefore, women begin to see a man's net worth as the first criterion for marriage. If a man isn't considered wealthy, some women discount him as a person. As more and more women work and have flourishing careers, it can become even more difficult—for both men and women. Men may feel the need to compete, to make as much or more money than the woman. Women might have trouble respecting a man who makes less money than she does.

When we push children to compete or to value the opposite sex for money, we are socially pulling males and females apart. The relationship is based on who makes more money as opposed to finances being mutually shared.

When a group of ten-year-olds were asked what they liked about a certain friend, most responded with, "Johnny has a swimming pool, lots of toys, a PlayStation, and a trampoline." Although this is not so shocking coming from ten-year-olds, a group of teens responded similarly when asked about a well-to-do friend. They liked Justine because she had great clothes that she let her friends borrow, a new car, a big house for parties, and an "in" at a local club. Not one person said they liked Justine for her personality, humor, or intelligence. This type of material-based attitude is pervasive in our society.

Not until we are faced with trauma or serious consequences do we reevaluate what is important in our lives—family, friends, our country. The priorities we establish in our day-to-day lives are what children will model. It is important to reflect on, and perhaps reassess, your priorities and then evaluate what privileges you are willing to give to your children.

Asking your child to give up a toy to charity or get fewer

birthday gifts or have a more modest party than a friend may seem difficult. You may ask, "Why should I give my child fewer material things if I can afford them?" Although every parent wants his child to have all that he can offer, this striving can give a child a false sense of power and leave the parent feeling angry and vulnerable. What is gained by the pursuit of things is a hollow existence, because it is a bottomless pit. A child will never feel satisfied, because there will always be more and more "things" to desire.

Giving a child every material thing should not be the goal of parenting. Parental goals are best centered around teaching a child values and responsibility, a love of learning, the arts, reading, and athletics, and how to establish good relationships. Somewhere in these pursuits, a child will find his way to something that excites or inspires him. In that, he will find success and happiness and even, perhaps, wealth.

Many people do not think about their priorities. We go about our daily lives influenced by other peoples' opinions, the media, and advertisers and never really reflect on what is important to ourselves and our families. You might be shocked to find out what your child's priorities are.

The following chart will help you to explore your priorities and give you a forum to discuss what really matters and put it into perspective. Ask your child what is important to him. See if he is mirroring your beliefs. Also, ask yourself what you would be willing to change.

PRIORITY CHART

List in order of importance your top five priorities:

1. _____

2. _____

3. _____

4. _____

5. _____

Ask your child, "What are your top five priorities?"

1. _____

2. _____

3. _____

4. _____

5. _____

What do you do (or what *can* you do) daily to nurture these priorities, change them, or reorder them? For example, if spending time with your children is a priority, ask yourself, "How much time *do I really* spend with my children? How can I create more time with them?"

What are you willing to give up to get more out of your life that is meaningful? Will you give up a tennis game to be with your children? Will you stay one hour less at the office to visit your parents or to do a charitable act? Start small; one hour a week is a good beginning to reprioritize your life and emphasize caring over competition.

There are no rewards for being a good person. There are no crowns or trophies. Crowns and trophies are momentary. They are fleeting symbols. Goodness lasts a lifetime. The rewards of leading a valuable life are long lasting. They are internal—not external. They can be felt, not seen. They do not sit on a shelf but rather in your heart and mind. The rewards of goodness cost nothing and can't be bought with money or influence. They don't come cheap, but are earned over a lifetime.

7

THE BURNED-OUT CHILD

The Burned-Out Child

Like a machine, human beings can break down. But children are thought to be resilient—capable of many physical and mental challenges. After all, children don't have the same stressors as adults, right? Unfortunately, this is no longer the case in present-day society. Children now carry bigger burdens on their shoulders. They are the burdens of expectations, and they can wear down the strongest shoulders because very few of us can meet all of the overinflated expectations of schools, our parents, society. The stressors of day-to-day existence—and the pressure to compete—can cause even the most confident child to break down. Sure, some youngsters are able to tolerate competitive pressure, but many simply can't handle it. The stressors of having to look great, be smart, achieve, be popular, and win at all costs will burn children out.

The burnout may come slowly, marked by an unusually cranky attitude, feigned illness, stomachaches. Or it can come with a bang: an eating disorder, a mental breakdown, or a complete shutdown from school and all activities. Children, as resilient as they are, have breaking points. Sometimes we fail to see the signs of child burnout because we simply can't imagine that an active child with good grades would have any worries or problems. But parents need to take notice. Some children may actually try to hide their distress because they don't want to upset their parents. But any child who is engaged in school and getting straight A's and is involved in sports, modeling, and dance recitals is competing. Even a child who may not be doing well academically is stressed because he feels the pressure to get better grades, to compete with kids who are more driven. And competition, by its very nature, creates stress. We are always looking over our shoulders at someone who has more or is more successful.

Pay attention to the following symptoms. If your child displays three or more symptoms at one time, take note. Try to find out what may be the cause. Pull back on activities. Give your child "downtime" with nothing to do.

SYMPTOMS OF BURNOUT

SLEEP DISTURBANCES	• Sleeping too long or too little for a period of a week or more • Nightmares or sleepwalking
PHYSICAL DISTRESS	• Increased allergy attacks • Headaches • Asthma • Rashes or hives • Stomachaches
EMOTIONAL DISTRESS	• Crying • Whining • Yelling • Nail biting • Obsessive-compulsive behavior
SOCIAL DISTRESS	• Arguments and withdrawal from friends and social functions
EATING DISORDERS	• Weight gain—more than 5 to 10 pounds • Weight loss—more than 5 to 10 pounds
SCHOOL PROBLEMS	• Falling grades • Behavior problems with teachers

None of these symptoms necessarily signal burnout by themselves. But if the behavior is unusual, is combined with other symptoms, and continues for more than a week, then you should consult a doctor or a therapist to get a proper diagnosis and evaluation.

Self-Pushers

Eric, thirteen, had to win. No matter what he did, he had to be the best—get the A, the award, the top honor. If he lost, he became furious. His perfectionism caused Eric to fall into a depression, and when he didn't make the soccer team, he had a breakdown. Somewhere Eric picked up the message that if he was not the best, he was not okay. His parents tried to slow him down and did not chastise him for less-than-perfect performance, but Eric was not content to be average.

Sadly, some children place the burden of overaccomplishment on themselves. They are trapped by their own perfectionism. Yes, some self-pushing is good and necessary in order to set and accomplish goals. But self-pushers who are obsessive are never satisfied with their performance. There is always frustration for self-pushers who cannot find a level of acceptance for themselves. This type of child is either modeling parent behavior and demands or is genetically predisposed to obsessive-compulsive behavior. There is always an inner voice saying, "You are not good enough." Some children push themselves so hard that they never enjoy any of their accomplishments. They are trapped by the need to accomplish more and more. In these cases, it is up to the parent to slow down his child before there are serious consequences.

If your child is a self-pusher, take a long, honest look at yourself; your child may be modeling your behavior. Do you push yourself to be perfect? Are you always dieting because you're not thin enough? Do you work long hours because no matter how much success you attain, you're looking to rise to the next level? If so, you may be unconsciously creating "shoulds" for the child—setting, by example, the rules for how to perform. The child grows up thinking this is the "right" way to behave. The child will push himself too hard, not realizing that he is not developed enough to meet these standards. When he inevitably fails to live up to the "ideal" modeled for him, his self-esteem will suffer; he'll perceive himself as a failure. Worse yet for the child, he'll begin to worry that his parents will think less of him, be disappointed because of his inability to live up to their example. As a result, he'll push himself even harder or else withdraw completely, thinking if he can't be who his parents expect him to be, why bother at all?

Some parents, not necessarily meaning to, impose their desires for their children onto the youngsters. All children go through a phase of exploring the world around them, including people, relationships, and hobbies. Adults have pre-conceived ideas of what is good for their child, and in a genuine attempt to protect her, may steer her away from certain people and activities. But it is through exploration that the mind matures and is able to develop and know one's own feelings, thoughts, likes, and dislikes. If a child is programmed to meet only parent-driven goals, he will never have the opportunity to make personal choices and get to know himself. He will self-push to please others but not to satisfy his own needs.

A child's ego is formed partly by parental reflection. The young ego may not be strong enough to resist the parent, and thus your child may give in to your desires in order to please you. By constantly pleasing the parent, the child internalizes these demands and feels unworthy if the demands are not met.

Overparenting

Terri and Jenny's mother, Anna, was proud to announce that she had her girls signed up for soccer, computer classes, dance lessons, and singing lessons. The girls were also auditioning for modeling jobs and getting straight A's in school. Now, most parents would feel a ping of jealousy. How does she do it? But the question should be, why does she do it? Somehow parents got the notion that as long as their child is getting good grades, it is okay to have them involved in five other activities.

Ironically, Anna complained that she had no life. Everything she did was for her children. This "selfless" attitude was not the mark of a perfect mother. It indicated a mom who wanted to live her life through her children and felt that any reflection on them would be a direct reflection on her. They had to be it all and do it all.

Everything was fine as long as they were meeting Anna's expectations. But when eleven-year-old Jenny started to reject the plan set up for her, the trouble began. Jenny's grades dropped, her interest in soccer waned, and her blossoming breasts and body were no longer model material. Anna became angrier and angrier. She tried to put Jenny on a diet hoping she'd be thin enough to resume modeling. Anna bribed her into playing soccer, promising Jenny clothes and goodies. But Jenny wanted to be with her friends and just hang out. So Anna turned all her attention on nine-year-old Terri. She put more pressure on her. This was her only chance of having a "star" kid.

Jenny, despite her mother's anger and protests, became a happier, better-adjusted child. She gave up soccer and modeling. Her grades were A's and B's, and she danced for fun, not competitively. On the other hand, Terri, the "star" child, who would do anything to please her mother, had a complete burnout by the time she was twelve years old. She developed an eating disorder and was so filled with performance anxiety that she had to be put on medication.

Some parents feel certain that they know what's best for their child and voice this opinion openly. One mother made choices for her child and decided her daughter would learn to play the piano even though the girl openly said she disliked the piano. This type of parenting is a formula for failure. If the child refuses to play piano, she feels guilty and has a sense that she let her mother down. If she pushes herself to play well in order to please her mother, she may not receive any real joy in playing but rather feels pressure to perform so that her mother will be happy. Inevitably the child will resent her mother for pushing her into an activity she does not enjoy and finds no pleasure in.

This turn of events can happen in the best of families, but it is less likely to occur when a child is encouraged to follow her interests and do her best—not feel compelled to meet parental or societal expectations.

My daughter and I fought for years over her grades. I yelled and badgered her and sat with her for hours—sometimes "helping" with her homework too much. By the time she entered high school, I was burned out from all this "overparenting." I told her, "I am handing you your education. It belongs to you—not me any longer." To my surprise, her grades soared. She became diligent about her work and really took personal pride in projects. This change came about because she cared. She took ownership of her work. The consequences of her actions became internalized. My pushing did not accomplish the goal; only when she was ready did her grades turn around.

You should teach your child good study habits, take an interest in her work, and be available to support her, but you have to be willing to let your child do poorly until he begins to take personal pride in his work. If Johnny doesn't study and gets a D, it is his problem. He can't blame you for not making him study harder. Personal responsibility is a powerful parenting tool.

This might be a difficult message for some parents to hear. They overparent because they are concerned about their children. They want the best for them and fear that without their guidance their children will not do well enough, not achieve, not succeed. But parents need to realize that no amount of pushing can force a child to become what they think he should be. The child will eventually balk, especially as he reaches adolescence and is fighting for his own identity. If you push your child too hard, he'll push you away.

Rushing from one activity to another has become an American way of life. Children are hurried from school to practice to rehearsal to homework to studying, and on and on, on a continual treadmill. Giving yourself and your child permission to slow down is a challenge. When you slow down, you have time to reflect—to think—and to dream.

These mind activities are just as important to success as the constant rush to "do." In essence you are taking time to just "be." For your child, reflection and downtime are ways to recharge his mental batteries.

Parents are often fearful of a daydreaming child. But stories abound of the great creators and geniuses throughout history who would idle away the time daydreaming. Little did people know that brilliant ideas were forming. Einstein was considered an idle dreamer. So was Bill Gates. These kinds of minds need to be encouraged but not pushed.

The best way to slow a child down is by example. Parents rush around in a frenzy with kids in tow. This creates anxiety and pressure. To heal the mind, pull back from overparenting:

- Take a day every week to pull the plug. That means nothing mechanical (no TV, radio, computer).

- Go for a walk or a bike ride together.

- Cook together, do an art project, go for a ride in the country or to the beach.

- Let your child sleep late. Don't always wake him up at six A.M. for soccer, dance, karate, baseball, etc.

- Go with your kids to the library or bookstore.

- Read to each other.

- Have family talks; tell jokes. Exchange stories about grandparents and each other.

If a fertile mind is burned out, the child may shut down, lose motivation, and give up. Remember the Beatles song "*Let It Be*"—these are indeed words of wisdom. The mind needs to be still.

The Burned-Out Competitive Parent

There are no perfect parents! This is a declaration I make in every book I write because it needs to be heard over and over again. The journey of parenting is one of mistakes, challenges, awareness, forgiveness, and knowledge. A parent who tries to be perfect puts so much pressure on herself and her child that eventually she sets up a no-win situation—one ripe for burnout. The parent who strives for perfection inevitably creates a less-than-perfect child because it is impossible to meet the superparent's standards. So it is in your child's best interest to focus less on perfection and more on being a realistic and effective parent. A parent who burns out, especially the mother, loses perspective about what's important for her family. She tries to do it all—be it all—and when she can't, she heads for a breakdown. When the parent breaks down, the child no longer feels safe and secure. The thinking is, "If my parent falls apart, then I can, too, because my parent is supposed to be the strong one."

The competitive parent never stops long enough to see she is about to hit the "wall," and when she pushes herself too hard, she starts to feel, "What about me? I'm exhausted and no one helps me." This parent can become resentful because she sets aside her needs for her child's. If you push your child and he doesn't meet your demands, you get angry so you push harder, often putting further demands on yourself to host, donate, carpool, help, sacrifice, coach, and volunteer. This parent wants to be it all, hoping her child will follow by example.

The superparent has a need to create constant frenetic activity, which causes tension and a highly charged atmosphere. Most supercompetitive parents intimidate the normal, ordinary parent. Competitive parents want to run the book drive, chair the parent-teacher committee, coach the soccer team, and do all the driving from lesson to lesson. Then the "normal" parents feel the need to start pushing harder and become competitive.

Superparents, although seen by the community as wonderful and altruistic, are not always the most attentive parents. It may be necessary to look at who is gaining from all of this parental effort and if the child is getting the short end of the stick. Perhaps much of the supercompetitive parent's activities should be curtailed so she can spend more time with her child.

But there is only so much energy a person can sustain, both physically and mentally. You can only give until there is nothing left. Many parents view themselves as all-powerful—believing that no one can do as good a parenting job or be as capable. They are also not willing to let anyone think that they are not completely together. But once a parent hits burnout, she is no longer capable of functioning well.

One mother was afraid that if she stopped the insane pace, her child would fall apart—he would lose his competitive edge and fall behind the other children. This reasoning is faulty because as noted throughout this book, the frantic race of competition is useless if the mind and body are too tired and overstimulated. The same holds true for a parent who becomes tired and cranky. Parental burnout has many of the same symptoms as child burnout: short temper, exhaustion, inability to concentrate, depression, loss of appetite, and anxiety. If you reach burnout, you become useless to yourself and your family.

AVOIDING PARENTAL BURNOUT

- Be realistic about what you can and cannot accomplish. Some parents have unrealistic expectations not only that they can do it all, but that doing less signifies failure. These busy parents will volunteer for everything. Do not take on too many projects for yourself or your child. Focus only on the ones that are truly meaningful in your lives.

- Ask people to help you out—a friend, relative, neighbor, or coworker. Competitive people do not like to give up control to others. The attitude is, "I can do it better and faster." This may be true, but if you burn out, you won't be doing anything at all. Ask for help with your children, chores, and projects and reciprocate when you can. You might find working with other people more satisfying than competing alone.

- Get organized. Make lists. Manage your time. Most competitive people are fairly well organized. But for those who are scattered, get a box for each project and a notebook and datebook. Outline your schedule daily, weekly, and monthly. Wherever there are three or more things in one day, cut something out.

- Go on a short vacation—or a long one, if possible. There is nothing as renewing as a vacation. Time away will slow you down, help you relax and put your life in perspective. Try to go to a destination that does not require you to get on and off a bus or plane, shuffling from one location to another. Also, try to take a few days alone with your spouse or partner, especially if he or she is also a competitive person. Some R & R and taking stock of your life might be the most beneficial thing the two of you can do for each other and your children.

- Go to therapy if you are too stressed and confused. Burnout can signal more serious problems. Besides your physical health, your mental health can be greatly affected. You should be evaluated for depression and/or anxiety disorder. Joining a group of parents who are having similar pressures can help you to talk through your feelings.

- Keep a journal. Writing your thoughts down can be a cathartic experience. You may have pent-up emotions and feel like you are going to blow. Writing these feelings down is a good way to discharge negative thoughts. Certainly a journal is a better recipient for those than your child.

Hopefully, you have learned in this book that understanding, acceptance, and awareness are the keys to creating a healthier and more positive relationship with your child. Pushing a child too hard and too fast will most likely lead to a "break" on some level. Emotionally, mentally, or physically—something has to give way when you are pushed too hard. The symptoms may not show up immediately, but eventually, if a child's back is up against a wall, you will get resistance.

Whether self-made or resulting from outside pushing, the burned-out child needs to slow down, evaluate priorities, and have some fun. After all, he's still a child.

8

COMMUNICATION LINES

Talk, Talk, Talk

Fourteen-year-old Steve hated baseball. He just didn't have the nerve to tell his dad, Ernie. Ernie had been a varsity baseball player and had the same expectations for his son. Instead of talking to his father about his feelings, Steve pulled further and further away from his dad. When the relationship deteriorated to the point that Steve would hardly talk to his father, the two went to see a therapist. The therapist was able to extrapolate that Steve wanted out of baseball. When Ernie was told about his son's feelings, he simply said, "Why didn't Steve just communicate what he wanted?"

Simple? Yes. But look how long and painful this process was for Ernie and Steve. Parent-child communication is vital to a healthy relationship, but often overlooked as a "given." As children become tweens and teens, communication breaks down. Often, without realizing it, you do most of the talking and your child does the listening—if he hasn't already tuned you out.

As a child, I lived in a parental dictatorship. Children were raised to be seen and not heard. There was little democratic process. In fact, most parent-child communication in past generations was based on a dictatorial edict. A child was considered disrespectful if he overstepped his place and questioned his parents.

As times and the nature of family relationships changed, children not only wanted to be heard, they needed to be. There are so many complicated issues in our lives today that communication skills are needed to talk about sensitive societal and family issues. Parents need to be able to handle negative emotions that can accompany growing up. Most of all, open communication allows a parent to pick up on a child's feelings about the pressures of school, sports, and social interactions. Also, by listening to your child, you will be able to determine what activities your child has an interest in and perhaps talk honestly about his thoughts on competition.

One of the most difficult things to accomplish is good

communication with an adolescent child. Every issue seems to press "hot" buttons. The most benign question can be met with raised voices and temperamental outbursts. Teens are under such enormous pressure from academics, social expectations, and sports that the added pressure may cause an adolescent to shut you out.

When Gerry asked his fifteen-year-old son, Brad, to do something, he was met with, "In a minute." The minute never came for Brad, and he rarely would listen to his father's requests. Gerry would lose his temper at Brad's retort, since he knew it was meaningless. This dialogue became a negative pattern that repeated itself again and again. Gerry yelled and Brad tuned him out. They didn't have the communication tools to begin a productive dialogue. As a result, Gerry and Brad just keep on fighting and growing more distant every day.

Some parents get frustrated by a lack of communication and turn to anger. When Nancy's ten-year-old son didn't listen to her, she yelled at him, "Trying to talk with you is useless. You never listen. I'm not even going to bother." Nancy constantly criticized and pushed her son, and his only defense was to withdraw. Her anger didn't help the communication problem—it only made it worse.

Like many behaviors, communication becomes habitual. The more we fail to talk out our feelings and listen to one another, the more we fail to communicate and often misinterpret what the other person is saying. This is particularly pertinent to the competition race.

The very nature of competition requires good communication between teammates, coach and player, teacher and student, parent and child. If you can't communicate effectively, then you will constantly be frustrated. Not only do you need to learn to listen, but it's vital to learn to hear what is "really" being said by the other person.

The most important step to opening the lines of communication is both your willingness and your child's to make constructive changes. Communicating differently might feel awkward at first. You may even hear things that you don't like. But ultimately talking and really listening to one another will be a significant step in attaining a better relationship.

Hear Me

Many communication problems occur when people don't hear one another. When emotions are high, it is sometimes difficult to listen to what is really being said. Also, sometimes we don't want to hear what someone is saying. Four-year-old Melanie did not like her toddler class. She told her mom, Kim, but Kim discounted Melanie's protests, thinking that she was too young to know what she wanted and what was good for her. Also, Kim's friends all brought their children to the class, and Kim enjoyed the social time. One day the teacher wanted the kids to sit quietly for an hour and listen to songs and stories. Melanie, an active child, was bored and unhappy. She would have preferred going to the park or a gym class. As a result, Melanie acted out. Kim punished her, and the class became a miserable time for both mother and child. Kim's own desire to have Melanie be part of the class inhibited her willingness to hear and accept Melanie's own input on the matter.

Sometimes children say things to parents in indirect ways, but the cues are not picked up. Seven-year-old Sue disliked dance class. Every time she went to class, she got a tummy ache. Her mother started taking her to doctors, who determined that Sue seemed to just get tummy aches on Saturday mornings before dance class. The doctor was able to connect the tummy ache to the class. Although disappointed, Sue's mom finally let her quit dance class. Suddenly her tummy aches subsided. Sue had been afraid to tell her mom how she really felt, and her mom missed her nonverbal message.

As parents, we must also be careful of the messages we give our children. A parent who wants something of her child often conveys the message in a punitive or negative manner. Contrary to what some parents think, kids *do* hear what they say, although many will act indifferent as a defense. Negative verbal messages become ingrained. For instance, if you say, "I see you got a C on your test again," your child may hear, "You only got a C. How poor. You'll never do well. You are not very smart." The child may then feel pressured or nagged; and if this message is "heard" repeatedly, it will become ingrained, causing the child to believe that he is indeed stupid.

In an effort to get your child to do better, you may be sending a message, but your child hears it incorrectly. If a child is told, "You have to be the best," what he may hear is, "If you are not the best, you are not okay." The child hears a hidden meaning behind the words. Unfortunately, communication breaks down even more because the child doesn't know how to say, "I'm trying as hard as I can. Why can't you accept me for who I am?" Instead, the child may withdraw or try even harder, trying to please his parents at his own emotional expense.

Miscommunication can create hostilities based on wrong assumptions. A parent who takes an assertive role as the one who does the talking, gives the advice, and so on may expect the child to hear what he's really saying, but what you say and what they hear can be two different things.

Use these skills for more effective communication:

- Do not "attack" the other person for his choices or ideas. If your child wants to drop out of soccer to play the tuba, listen to his feelings and reasons. Don't put down his choice because it does not fit your desires.

- Let the other person complete what she has to say. Wait a minute before answering if it is a "hot" topic. Don't interrupt or let your child interrupt. Each person should count to ten before answering.

- Don't be impulsive. Think about what you want to communicate and frame your words positively. We tend to lash out at people when they say something contrary to our views. Think about how you would react if you were on the receiving end of what you are about to say. You get further with kind words.

- Be honest but not hurtful. If your child is not a great athlete, focus on the skills he does best, but don't lie and tell him he'd have Olympic potential if he worked harder.

- Pay attention and look the person in the eye. Let the person know you care about what he or she is saying, and you will communicate better. This skill develops empathy.

- Stay on the subject. Don't interrupt with stories about yourself. Let the other person talk about himself and complete his thoughts.

- Ask informed and caring questions. If your child is studying Shakespeare, try to get her to teach you something.

- Don't always give advice and your opinion. Try to develop give-and-take in your conversations. Not every subject calls for your opinion. Children can be extremely insightful. Listen to their advice and opinions.

Family Forum

One of the most effective ways to open the lines of communication is to hold family forums, in which family members can discuss their thoughts, feelings, problems, and concerns. The goal is to reach "an honest place" through a release of truthful feelings. For the competitive parent, it may be difficult to hear some truths, but for a loving parent, the truth is the only way to be a successful parent.

There are rules for the family forum. The forum is not a place to attack another person's vulnerabilities. Twelve-year-old Danny was sensitive about his not getting invited to a big party, and this came out at a family forum. His mother asked him a dozen questions: "Why do you think you weren't invited? Are you friendly with the girl who gave the party? Should I talk with her mother? . . ." Danny wanted to run and hide rather than sit and talk with his family about his social problems. The forum is a time to come together in a nonintrusive way. It's important that you sit, if possible, at a round table so your child doesn't feel he is being interrogated by two parents facing him.

Eleven-year-old Ellen was able to tell her mother, Kate, in a family forum that she didn't want to go to modeling auditions and beauty pageants. She felt like she was on display and was tired of thinking about her looks all the time. Ellen wanted to hang out with her friends on the weekends. Kate had a difficult time hearing this honesty from her daughter, but this information was revelational for Kate as well as cathartic for Ellen. Ellen and Kate became more open with one another and started a better relationship—one in which Ellen could express her feelings without reprisals or criticisms from Kate.

You can also present a "say something nice" roundtable. Each family member says something nice or what he likes about each person. This can be specific ("I liked when Dad helped me with my science project") or general ("I like that my sister lets me use her computer").

These skills help promote a positive attitude toward family and home as well as take the emphasis off of competition.

Ground Rules for a Family Forum

- Shut off the phones, the fax, the beepers, the computer.

- Each person talks for up to five minutes.

- Keep the forum to no less than twenty minutes and no more than an hour.

- Try to pick the same time each week.

- Do not judge what each person says. Really.

- Do not interrupt the person speaking.

- Try not to become defensive.

- Do not criticize how feelings are expressed.

- Three negative remarks stop the meeting.

- One person should guide and facilitate, track time, mediate angry comments. Alternate and let your child be the one in charge.

Family Problem Solving

When you have learned to communicate better, you will need skills to help your child (and family) solve problems. Problem-solving tools can encourage cooperation among family members and prevent negative input. During a family meeting, members can brainstorm together to try to find solutions to problems. Try to stay goal-oriented rather than identifying negative behavior. For example, don't talk about your teenage daughter's weight or your son's laziness every time you have a meeting.

Parents often wait until there are strong, angry feelings before they discuss a problem. This is the worst way to go about it. If you are angry and you approach your child with angry feelings, he will become defensive or shut down. You want to try to identify and solve problems early on.

The following gives positive ways to initiate such a discussion with your child:

Positive Ways to Approach Issues with Your Child

- Approach your child at an appropriate time, not when you are both in a hurry, and not in the heat of anger. Busy parents often "discipline on the run," and the problem escalates. You don't solve problems when you are upset.

- Sit down. Take time without interruptions—phones ringing, appointments, classes. Unplug everything.

- Decide who should talk to your child. If you are too combustible, maybe another family member should approach the subject. I'm the designated talker; my husband gets way too upset. Both parents can overwhelm some children.

- Think about what you want to say. Don't attack.

- Do not criticize, scream and yell, or be sarcastic. These tactics usually get you nowhere. Kids will tune out, cry, scream back, or walk away.

- Try to be calm and nurturing. Better yet, try using humor. If you can neutralize a situation with humor, you have a better chance of being heard. For instance, say, "So you drove your bike through Mrs. Abrams's really ugly flower garden? Now, even though it's an eyesore, that is not the way to act. Go apologize and offer to plant her some new flowers."

The following steps are the basic rules for problem solving. No rules are set in stone, but they can help get you through difficult family situations.

RULES FOR PROBLEM SOLVING

- Let everyone participate in defining the problem. You will be surprised to see that everyone may view a problem differently.

- Write down all suggested solutions, without endorsing or negating anyone's ideas. Some way-out suggestions may ultimately turn out to be the answer.

- Avoid criticism or hostility. This creates an angry forum. If you do start to argue, everyone take a ten-minute time-out to cool down. There is no right or wrong. It is a collaborative effort—so everyone needs to agree. If you get angry because you only see your side, you have solved nothing.

- Once you and your child have written down all possible solutions, evaluate them. Eliminate suggestions that clearly won't work.

- Find a solution that is fair and agreeable to everyone. Be willing to compromise. This is the most important point. If your child tells you she doesn't want to play soccer anymore, compromise—invite her to explore another activity she thinks she might like better.

- Put your plan into action. If your solution doesn't work, try an alternative. Be willing to make changes and go back and reevaluate what's working and what's not.

If you teach your child these skills, you will be giving him tools he can use his entire life. By working together to be open and fair, solve problems, and release feelings, you turn negativity into positive parenting.

You are now heading toward the finish line. Perhaps the finish is the most difficult because it asks you to take the hardest and most realistic look at yourself and then make changes. Change for many of us is difficult. Try to think of the finish as a challenge—a competition, if you must—to become a more effective and thoughtful parent.

9

THE FINISH LINE

And the Winner Is . . .

There are no real winners in the competition race because in life the finish line moves constantly. There will always be a new winner because someone smarter, prettier, and more talented will inevitably come along. The ability to learn, change, grow, accept, forgive, and begin again are the markers of each new start. The strong relationship you create with your child should become the constant that you strive for. To raise a happy, self-confident, and independent-thinking person is the measure of success, not how many A's or trophies your child accumulates.

Now that we've shown how destructive certain types of competitive pushing can be, there are ways to help your child become a more successful person by taking off the pressure, helping to stimulate his creativity, focusing on his positive traits, and opening up the lines of communication. Most important is to model the type of behaviors that you want your child to emulate. You are the mirror to your child—his first teacher. He watches everything you say and do. The way he treats people, his manners, his humanity—are all learned from his parents. Although it is normal for a child to pull away from his parent during crucial times of adolescent growth, he will take the lessons he learned and integrate them into his behavior.

Letting Go of Expectations

The anxiety level of parenting is off the chart. There is such a high bar raised for children, and those who cannot meet these expectations are immediately tested for learning problems so they can receive accommodations. The word "gifted," which generally refers to a child who meets certain IQ and academic standards, seems to apply to the majority of children today. Parents rattle off children's scores like merit badges. In previous generations, scores and special circumstances were private family matters. But not anymore. Parents boast about their children's accomplishments because they think it makes them look like good parents. But the intertwining of parent and child egos can be like a noose. If you impose your goals and expectations on your child, and make his performance responsible for how you feel about yourself, you may strangle your child's sense of self; he'll spend all his energy trying to achieve your goals and please you, instead of worrying about his own needs and desires.

Many parents who are driven by their own internal ambitions refuse to believe that they may have a different kind of child—one who is not ambitious or competitive. But by now, you should have a clearer picture of how your child learns, what his strengths and weaknesses are, and how he handles competition. What you want for your child may be counterproductive to his dreams and talents. By building expectations of your child that are based on the expectations you place on yourself, you are setting him up to fail. Your dreams cannot become your child's because you are two different people.

Derrick was a straight A student. He went to Stanford and became a successful lawyer like his own father. Derrick's son, Justin, performed poorly in school and was diagnosed with attention deficit disorder at the age of eight. Derrick could not accept this fact, even though it was evident that Justin was trying but failing to focus and concentrate on his schoolwork. It was suggested Justin repeat third grade, but Derrick would not hear of it and refused to concede that *his* son had a problem. He blamed everyone—the school, the teachers, even his wife—for being "too easy" on Justin. Derrick yelled at Justin, badgered him about his work. He even placed the expectation on Justin that someday he would go to Stanford and become a lawyer. Derrick was furious that Justin's work was sloppy and incomplete. Even though Justin was trying, Derrick accused him of being lazy.

By seventh grade, Justin was barely passing. Derrick constantly reminded Justin of what a good student he had been and expected the same of his son. Eventually Justin, feeling he could never live up to his father's expectations, stopped trying. He failed eighth grade, and was left back. This took some of the pressure off of Justin. He was able to work at a slower pace.

Sadly, parents who are unwilling to let go of their high expectations stand to suffer years of disappointment. The parent's disappointment is then transferred to his child, who goes through life feeling responsible for his parent's unhappiness. Ultimately it is the child who suffers because he can never feel good enough about himself.

Build Internal Structures

Some parents might say, "If you don't have high expectations for your child, then he won't try to do his best." But this theory is faulty. It shortchanges your child, whose internal ego structures—that is, his sense of self—are built by supporting, not dictating or pushing, your child's choices and feelings. Self-esteem is nurtured by helping your child create and support *his* view of himself—not just your view. With a strong internal structure, your child will be able to withstand negative input from external sources (peers, coaches, media, etc.) because the child believes he is worthwhile and is not overly vulnerable and sensitive.

My friend Becky confessed that when she was a child, she got the message, "You are not okay." She was shy and afraid to try new things because she thought that she wasn't quite good enough, smart enough, pretty enough. If she couldn't compete, then she felt she wasn't worthwhile. She always made a decision based on noncompetition. She naturally thought she would lose, come in second, not get the job. It took years of therapy and the loving acceptance of friends and her husband to give her the confidence to move forward with both a career and intimate relationships.

When I grew up, I constantly looked to my parents for validation. Without their approval, I couldn't move forward. I was hesitant to attempt new tasks and projects because I was afraid to fail. I didn't want to disappoint my parents. Breaking free of their psychological hold on me was an arduous task. I had to reparent myself—accepting my positive and negative traits.

Parenting is a balancing act between teaching and guiding

your child and letting him forge his own path. Parents must resist the urge to push too hard and try to control their children's behavior. Instead, they must let them make mistakes and ultimately attain a sense of confidence and autonomy. It is imperative that no matter what, the outcome belongs to the child.

The Sibling Sprint

Siblings and competition go hand in hand. The impact of families competing can have long-term effects on children. The relationship established between siblings affects their views of themselves into adulthood. Although some may argue that the success of one sibling has nothing to do with the failure of another, the contrary seems to be true. Some children are so competitive, talented, and high-powered that an enormous amount of their parents' energy comes to them at the expense of the others. One mother proclaimed that her older son was "the star." He got perfect grades, was a top athlete, and was very popular. Her younger son struggled with everything, and although she constantly urged him to follow his brother's example, it was to no avail. The young boy grew up in his brother's shadow and believed that he could never compete even though he tried. He felt that he was the brother who was a failure and led his life accordingly.

It is easy for siblings to become externally focused because of the labels that are attached to children. They only see their siblings as others view them—the smart sister, the talented brother. They see themselves as the dumb little brother, the plain sister, the clumsy kid. By living in the same household with someone positively labeled, negative images are constantly reinforced. Some children actually act out in order to get attention. If they can't compete, at least someone will take notice even if the behavior is inappropriate.

Carol always acted like the clown in her family because she felt she could never compete with her sister's beauty. Sandy received a lot of attention because she was so poised and pretty. In order for Carol to feel worthwhile, she would pull pranks. She'd get in trouble, but at least she got attention.

When a child is directed to look at his internal strengths, he is less apt to compete and more likely to focus on achieving for himself. Here are some guidelines for parents to diminish sibling rivalry and help their children develop internal strengths:

- Love and treat your children equally.

- Never make comparisons between children.

- Do not label your children ("the smart one," "the athletic one").

- Do not use your children to gain affection for yourself by testing how much each loves you.

- Encourage cooperation, not competition.

- Instill family loyalty and a "brother helping brother" attitude.

Perhaps the most important way to prevent sibling rivalry is to nurture the positive traits in your children and have a belief that each child has some special gift.

Nurturing Creativity

A parent who refuses to slow the pace of the competition race can actually be self-defeating in her efforts to help her child. Success can be stifled when a child is restricted in his creative expression. More often than not, some schools use music, art, and drama as "throwaway" classes. Only academics are seen as important. Parents buy into the myth that creative pursuits are frivolous extras and push their children to expend all of their energy in academic pursuits. When children are nursery school age, parents are immediately anxious if their toddlers are not learning words, colors, or numbers. Some demand that their little ones start to read and write before they are in kindergarten. Many pre-K classes have actually assigned homework to tots barely out of diapers. But this focus on academics does not serve the child well. A child's creativity needs to be nurtured. Teaching a child "the three R's" will certainly serve her well, but what we really need to do is encourage our children to think. We need to spark their curiosity, unleash their natural instinct to explore, and lead them to discover the world around them. We need to help them tap into their innate creativity.

The key element in nurturing creativity is to allow your child the freedom and the time to pursue play and his interests. According to psychologist Dr. Jill Model Barth, "Unstructured play allows the mind to be still, and out of a still mind develops the creative process." Dr. Barth goes on to explain, "If there is always something stimulating the mind, the child becomes scattered and overstimulated. This leads to frustration."

Because parents overschedule and structure every minute of their child's day, many children have no free time. Children are pushed to grow up fast and constantly learn. But all this academic learning can lead to a failed mind and an empty heart.

Many children do not have the freedom to develop because their time is forever filled up with activities. Parents schedule children in one activity after the other. Children who can get lost for hours in one activity have enough time to fully explore it. It is this exploration that leads to learning. But if a child is pushed along from one activity to the next, he is unable to really focus his attention. As soon as a child is beginning to get involved in something, the bell rings, the practice is over, it's time to move on. The child barely has time to absorb what he just experienced. He certainly doesn't have time to discover something new.

Encouraging creativity does not mean enrolling your child in art class and buying her an easel and a set of oil paints. Creativity means thinking in new ways, discovering new ideas. Yes, the fine arts can be a wonderful way to tap into creativity, but they should be fun. Young children shouldn't be "taught" how to be creative. It's ludicrous to grade children's creative pursuits. How frustrating for an eight- or nine-year-old to receive a C because he can't draw lines and angles like a professional. All children's art should be considered beautiful expressions of themselves. Evaluating a child's creative endeavors makes him feel devalued. Comparisons to a master's or even other children's "better" efforts will kill the drive toward creativity. A child's creativity should be encouraged without the fear of grades.

The same applies to interest in a particular subject that excites your child. If your child expresses a love of music, don't rush to sign him up for piano lessons. If your six-year-old child likes the stars, that doesn't mean he's going to be a scientist; and don't feel compelled to register him in science classes five days a week. You can support your child's interest in a subject even if you know little about it. If you know nothing about the subject, then find someone who does. Or go to the library and check out a book. Your child's interest in the subject may be short-lived, but give him a chance to explore at his own pace and in his own time. Let his natural curiosity lead him and be there to support his creative endeavors.

As parents, we should strive to stimulate our children's creative instincts. We must make a conscious effort to not inhibit them. Many things may stifle children and push them away from their natural inclinations to enjoy learning and the creative process. According to Dr. Teresa Amabile, a well-known researcher on creativity and author of *Creativity in Context,* these are some creativity killers:

- *Surveillance.* Do not hover over children. This makes them feel uncomfortable. If a child is constantly being observed, he is unlikely to take creative chances.

- *Evaluation.* If you judge what a child creates, he will become unwilling to take risks and will create only to please the parent or teacher.

- *Rewards.* Prizes—such as trophies, money, or stars—if overused, will deprive a child of the intrinsic pleasure of creativity. His goal will be for the prize and not the creative outcome.

- *Competition.* By placing a child in a win-lose situation, someone will come out on the bottom and surely feel unworthy. Creative pursuits, rather than competitive ones, encourage children to progress at their own pace.

- *Overcontrol.* Telling children how to do things—their schoolwork, play, chores—leaves them feeling disempowered. A child feels fearful that any originality will be wrong.

- *Restricted choices.* By making all of your child's decisions and not allowing him to follow his own curiosity, he may lose interest, rebel, or simply overcomply.

- *Pressure.* Placing too high expectations on a child's ability to perform actually backfires. Children may end up having an aversion to the very thing you are trying to encourage.

If you want your child to be creative at an early age, then let him play. Play lets children "let off steam" and stimulates creative thinking. Play also helps children be socially adapted, according to famed educator Maria Montessori, whose ideas revolve around the educational philosophy that play is the child's "work." Group play is a free-form way to learn to share rather than compete—to use teamwork.

If play is geared to have a winner all the time, then a child can become anxious and feel inhibited. Why can't play just be play? Toys that ignite the imagination, like Legos, blocks, and art materials, stimulate expression. Parents should allow a child's natural creative inclinations to surface and the child to explore freely.

Mirror Images

In order to develop into a healthy person, it is vital that a child have a belief in his or her own ability. Self-confidence in a child starts with the parents. If you act confidently and display a belief in your child, he will most likely follow suit. Parents are a child's first mirror. He sees himself through his parents' eyes; he knows he is good when his parents smile, and he feels ashamed of himself when he sees them frown. As the child grows, the parent mirrors back the message, "You are okay," or "You are not okay." The child can doubt his abilities if the parent is constantly critical and belittling.

Dena told her daughter, Amy, from the time the child could write numbers, that she was poor in math. It wasn't personal—Dena said everyone in their family had problems with numbers. As a result, Amy continued the pattern. She got D's and F's in math all through school. She believed her mother and put little effort in trying to become a better math student. "I'll never do well in math," she thought, "so why try." Finally Amy was lucky enough to have a teacher who believed Amy could do well in math. He worked with her and convinced Amy that she had no math block. As a result, she received her first ever A in math. This A turned Amy's mother around. She too had believed she could never achieve in math because of what her own parents had told her, but now she saw that belief in one's own ability could break the pattern.

Parental patterns are, for the most part, conditioned into our personalities by our own upbringing. Modeling, the strongest of all personality imprinting, is how we copy our parents' behavior. You may have unconsciously acquired your father's way of talking with his hands of your mother's habit of biting her lip when nervous.

Subsequently, the way you behave will, in part, determine how your child behaves. A child will model both positive and negative aspects of his parents' behavior. Young girls start to emulate their mothers early on. They will pretend to apply lipstick, style their hair, and play dress-up. Boys may pretend to shave.

Psychological modeling has an even bigger impact on children. This type of modeling affects the things we say to our child, which in turn contribute to the formation of his character. For example, Andy's father, Jim, grew up in a household full of pessimists. Jim's parents suffered a great deal in their lives and came to believe that bad things would always befall them. Whenever Jim would compete in any event, they gave him no support. In fact, they gave him subtle—and sometimes not so subtle—messages that he probably wouldn't win. Eventually he stopped trying, since he believed he wouldn't win anyway. He has carried this sense of futility into adulthood, and now gives the same messages to Andy. Even though his friends urged him to try out for the track team, Andy wouldn't. He "knew" he would never make it.

A child will mirror the parental model. He needs to feel safe and validated by what he sees, hears, and experiences. Therefore, it is important to model positive behaviors, especially with young children. Good modeling creates a strong sense of self-worth.

Healthy Competition

Competition can have a positive side, and parents can promote healthy competition. "Healthy competition starts with a child that is focused on bettering himself for his own satisfaction and enjoyment," says psychologist Terry Gopadze. Healthy competition is fostered by a parent who helps his child focus on long-term goals as opposed to "evaluating himself or others on a daily basis."

It is important that children enjoy what they are doing and learning even if they are not successful in accomplishing an external goal. According to Gopadze, "Encouraging children to be compassionate with themselves and others through wins and losses can be the most effective way to teach healthy competition."

One of the most difficult lessons in competitiveness is accepting the outcome and being able to acknowledge superior quality in one's peers. Ten-year-old Steven couldn't stand to lose at anything. He would have temper tantrums if he lost at a game or a sport. His father reacted similarly; Steven witnessed his dad throwing his tennis racket a number of times after a loss. This type of negative modeling is the antithesis of healthy competition.

Perhaps the best example of healthy competition is the way some of the athletes competed at the 2002 Winter Olympics. These young athletes showed more sportsmanship, humility, and maturity than the adults—the judges, the Olympic committee members, and the media. Figure skaters Irina Slutskaya, David Pelletier, and Jamie Sale were all magnificent in the way they competed. They understood that their goal was to skate to attain a personal best—not just to focus on the medals. The media tried to kick up a firestorm among the athletes, but the healthy competitors refused to fall prey to this tactic. They showed grace and class amid adult screams and protests.

According to Dr. Harvey L. Ruben in his book *Competing,* competition can be a positive force, "a way of validating ourselves, of reinforcing our sense not only of survival but of self-worth and dignity. The development of a healthy ego," Ruben asserts, "depends on learning how to manage the competitive interactions between ourselves and other people."

These interactions must be rooted in reality. For instance, a child who has never hit a baseball may have trouble competing with a child who has been in Little League for five years. Just wanting to, or just being athletic, may not be enough to compete.

There are ways to help your child compete in a healthy way. First, it is important to evaluate your child's strengths. That is not to say there are not exceptions, but to push a child to do something he is not prepared for can set him up for failure. Many parents see a toddler throw a ball and immediately want to get him a personal coach. Wait and see what activities your child gravitates to, and let him explore his interests.

Preparation is so important to any goal. Teach your child that reaching a goal is a process. Success doesn't usually happen overnight. Practice and perseverence are steps that lead to achievement. If your child wants to be on a dance team, get her involved with classes in various types of dance and let her be taught by a professional. You will know within a few years if your child has the talent and drive to keep dancing at a higher level. Her teachers will tell you and so will she.

Last, have the correct equipment. That could mean properly fitted soccer shoes or a baseball glove, dance shoes, or a piano. Whatever the competition, have appropriate tools. You don't have to have the most expensive tools, especially for a child, but the right tools are essential.

Also, if your child keeps losing at something, be open to having him try things a little bit differently. When we are willing to change, amazing things can happen.

Reality Checklist

In order to have a child who is a healthy competitor, it is important to make realistic assessments. The following reality checklist will help you to set realistic expectations for your child.

- What are your child's best qualities? When you assess your child's qualities, make sure you consider personality traits such as generosity, fairness, and kindness. All these things help to create a healthy competitor.

- What are your child's weaknesses? Try not to be punitive but rather realistic. Does your child's bad temper or bossiness get in his way?

- Do you push your child into areas that you like and he doesn't?

- Do you listen to your child? Children will express their feelings if you give them an open forum. Don't discount what your child tells you.

- Set goals that are not out of reach, but attainable. Every parent wants straight A's, but that is not always possible. Be fair to your child. Set small goals and give positive reinforcement for even the tiniest amount of progress.

- Assess your child's progress and decide if you overestimated his talents.

- Do you respect your child's personal goals and allow him to compete in his own way? Some children will never have the competitive drive that you would like.

- Do you help your child to accept both winning and losing? This is the most important point. Losing with grace and humility is as important as winning. Both create a framework for good character by teaching us to accept the ups and downs of life and then to move forward.

10

COOL DOWN

As a parent, you have certain expectations of how your child should be. You expect him to try his best, to be successful, to compete. But not every child can be all his parents want him to be. You may be disappointed and not approve of your child's choices. The expectations of what you think your child "should be" may be different from what he actually is. Each human being creates a different life experience. The most difficult aspect of life is accepting differences in each other, especially our children.

Pushed to the Edge may have angered or enlightened you, but hopefully, it has brought you to an understanding of the meaning of child competition and how it impacts the parent-child relationship. Awareness of who you are as a parent and what you want to become is the first step toward stopping the competition race, a race that few can win because the bar will forever be raised higher.

You must be careful not to withdraw from a child who does not live up to your expectations. A parent emotionally isolates a child by withdrawing love. Pulling away your love and attention is perhaps the cruelest thing you can do to your child. Your child needs your trust and strong parental bonds. The way to stop emotional isolation is to be accepting. By putting your child first and the outcome of his competition second, you begin the process of strengthening and renewing your relationship with him. To begin this process, you must be honest about yourself and your parenting approach as well as have a realistic assessment of your child and his abilities. Hopefully this book has given you the tools to embrace that honestly.

No two people are the same, and each person will parent differently because there are so many variables in our personalities and behavior. Each of us approaches competition in our own way. If you did identify strongly with a particular chapter, then you may want to focus on that aspect of competition. You may only want to choose the techniques that work for you and your family.

Understanding

The key to changing the parent-child relationship is understanding. By making fewer demands on your child to constantly perform at a certain level, you will be able to get your child to listen to you. If you back him up against a wall and push too hard, you will get resistance.

Danielle was crazed because her teenage daughter, Joy, did not go out every weekend. Danielle's friends bragged about their gregarious, popular girls, which made Danielle more and more anxious about Joy's introversion. Danielle was envious of her friends' children and their popularity. Danielle decided to throw a party and encouraged Joy to invite all the "popular" kids. But Joy was uninterested; she enjoyed staying at home. The party did not turn out well, and many of the so-called popular kids did not attend. This only alienated Joy further from the kids she did not identify with. Her mom pushed her to socialize and this caused a rift between the mother and daughter.

Danielle was intent on pushing her daughter into a social situation that she wanted, but Joy didn't. This is where honest assessment is valuable. Danielle needs to see Joy for who she really is. Joy needs to be aware of her mother's feelings, and perhaps Danielle can share some of her own teenage experiences with Joy. Danielle may have been unpopular or shy as a teen. Maybe she wants a different experience for her child. Or maybe Danielle was very popular and cannot stand the fact that her daughter is the opposite. But Danielle must understand that she cannot change Joy's nature any more than she could change her own. Danielle must also understand that love and success are not measured by teenage popularity.

When parent and child understand each other the pushing and resenting can stop, and both parent and child can appreciate the other and be true to themselves.

Forgive, Don't Forget

It is unrealistic to think that after reading this book you will no longer be a competitive parent. The ultimate goal here is to learn to know your child, accept him, work within the parameters of his strengths and weaknesses, and stop pushing him into areas that are clearly your interests and not his. Hopefully you will be able to find new ways to relate to your child, and you'll be more cognizant of the motives that cause you to push too hard too fast. You have to be willing to forgive yourself for past or present mistakes. Much of what we do is unconscious—a by-product of our own upbringing and how we reflect society's influence. Anger at yourself or past experiences will only hinder the chances to grow and change emotionally, therefore further impacting your child.

For this reason, it is important to forgive yourself, your parents, and society, and to take personal responsibility for any negative actions. Forgiving yourself is complex because it means coming to terms with your own anger and dissatisfaction. It means admitting mistakes and forgiving your child for not always meeting your expectations and the expectations of others. But breaking the pattern of pushing and negative parenting must begin with forgiveness.

You may have trouble with the notion of forgiveness—even balk at the very idea. But by forgiving yourself for being an imperfect parent, you are admitting you are fallible and human and you are setting the stage for a healthier relationship with your child. You must also ask your child to forgive you for pushing him to the edge and for not accepting him unconditionally.

After you forgive, don't forget. Never forget what is important and meaningful in your life. The key point of this book is to remind you of the value of your child and how compromising those values by pushing her to be overcompetitive can have a negative result. By forgetting what is meaningful, you create tension and pressure. Children should enjoy childhood. It should be a time of exploration. Never forget to have fun. Be silly, laugh, do unexpected things, and relax. Those are the moments that will build memories for your child.

A highly successful businessman I know has three amazing, bright, successful children. I asked my friend what his parenting secret was. He laughed and said that there was no secret. They could have been given everything financially and pushed to compete with the elite in society, but instead his children went to public school, got jobs at sixteen, performed community service as a family, played sports for fun, and each one chose a path that reflected his or her own choices. Their father supported their passions without judgment, but expected each child to stand on his or her own feet financially after college.

These children had always felt "safe" to explore who they were and what they wanted. Without the intense pressure to compete, they could "smell the roses." Life was filled with endless possibilities. This father's secret was never forgetting to see his children as separate individuals—each one unique—and to respect their differences and support them.

Some great tools for parenting success are listed below. These are basic rules that should be used all through life.

Tools for Parenting Success

- Spend time with your kids having fun.

- Teach manners and etiquette.

- Have family talks once a week without interruption.

- Allow your children to come to their own decisions about what activities they want to participate in.

- Be a positive role model.

- Have a set of values to live by.

These parenting tools may seem obvious, but with the stress placed on the family to be, to go, to do, and to constantly compete, we all lose sight of what is truly important at some time or another. It is often the things in our lives that we take for granted—our relationship with our children—that can slip through our fingers. The work you do as a parent is the most important thing you will ever do in life. Make these tools a priority. You'll all end up winners!

EPILOGUE

The journey of parenting can take us to some dark and frightening places. We can find ourselves questioning everything we know and wondering what we are doing wrong. The best, most loving parents make mistakes. That's because there is no infallible formula for being a parent.

Yes, I have stressed good role modeling, positive reinforcement, encouragement, values, unconditional love, and communication. But you can do all of these things and still make mistakes and struggle with parenthood. The reason for the difficulties is a simple one: Parents are human. We stumble over our own desire to give everything to our children and, in doing so, compromise our value system. We believe in good sportsmanship, but in the race to make our children number one, we may forget about fair play and honesty. We covet beauty and physical perfection, but in this quest we may turn our children into sexualized objects. None of us do this to hurt our children, because I truly believe every parent acts out of love. But acting out of love is sometimes misguided. However, our mistakes and our struggles help us learn and arrive at smart, conscious decisions.

The one rule we must all follow is to give our children our unconditional love. Unconditional love comes with no strings—good or bad, pretty or plain, strong or weak, smart or simple, a child must be accepted as is.

Competition will never cease. It is part of human nature. It is the degree to which we compete and how we win and lose that separate us as individuals. The rules of competition are yours to teach to your child. You have the challenge to direct your child to enjoy the process, not just the product; to stress personality over prettiness; to be one of the team, not always number one; and to compete with fairness, not fights.

Ultimately, your child should be encouraged, guided, and disciplined. Listen to your child. He knows his limits and liabilities. He will signal in many ways when he has been pushed too far. Respect his thoughts and feelings, and respect him for who he is. With the right approach, unconditional love, and understanding, every child and every parent can be a winner.

Donna G. Corwin is the author of seven parenting psychology books and more than three hundred articles that have appeared in magazines such as *Parenting, Child Magazine, Working Woman, Working Mother, Shape, Parents, L.A. Parent,* and *Los Angeles Family.* She has appeared on numerous television and radio shows and is a guest lecturer on parenting for the Motion Picture Wellness Program. Ms. Corwin lives in Beverly Hills, California, with her husband, Stan, and their daughter, Alexandra.